GUIDEBOOK FOR VISITING

VIENNA

WITH A MAP OF THE CITY

115 COLOUR ILLUSTRATIONS

BONECHI VERLAG STYRIA

Vertrieb
für Österreich
VERLAG STYRIA
A 8010 GRAZ, Schönaugasse 64

für die Bundesrepublik Deutschland
VERLAG STYRIA
D 5000 Köln 51, Schillerstrasse 6

Printed in Italy by Centro Stampa Editoriale Bonechi.

Photographs from the Publisher's Archives.
Photographers:

MARCO BANTI
Pages 14 (right); 17 (left); 26; 31 (below); 32; 35; 38
(right); 43; 44; 48 (right); 79 (right); 80; 81 (left); 84;
85 (above and below left); 92 (above and below
left); 94 (above).

ALESSANDRO DEL CONTE
Pages 35 (left); 47; 81 (right); 89.

LUIGI DI GIOVINE
Pages 39; 45 (above); 61; 63; 64; 67; 68; 69; 70; 71
(below); 75; 78 (left); 91; 94 (below); 95 (above).

FOTOSTUDIO OTTO
Pages 12; 13; 14 (left); 16; 17 (right); 19; 21; 22; 24;
25; 27; 28; 29; 33; 37; 38 (left); 40; 41; 42; 45
(below); 46; 48 (left); 52; 62; 65; 71 (above); 72; 73;
74; 76; 77; 78 (above); 79; 83; 88; 93; 95.

PHOTO MEYER
Pages 53; 54; 55; 56; 59; 60; 92 (right).

PIERO ROSI
Pages 23; 30 (above); 35 (right); 49; 50; 58; 66; 87.

We are indebted for the kind permission to:
Bundesministerium für Land-und Forstwirtschaft Wien
Hofburg Burghauptmannschaft Wien
Kunsthistorisches Museum Wien
Österreichische Galerie im Belvedere Wien
Schlosshauptmannschaft Schönbrunn Wien

Translation by Erika PAULI

ISBN 3 222 11757 8

As the Romans marched northwards hoping to extend the frontiers of the Empire all the way to the Elbe river, they reached the site of the present-day city of Vienna. At the time it was inhabited by a Celtic peoples who had dominated the area four or five centuries earlier, replacing an older Veneto-Illyrian population. Recent excavations in the area have brought to light objects from the Neolithic period, proof of the fact that people were already living here 3000 years before the birth of Christ. As soon as the Romans realized the strategic importance of the Celtic settlement, they built a fortified military camp. The powerful Xth legion was stationed here for three centuries, beginning with the middle of the 1st century A.D. The name of the camp, Vindobona, may derive from the Celtic word Vindomina, or Vindo, which means white and which probably alludes to the city's ancient splendor. The specific task of this encampment was to defend the province of Pannonia from incursions by the warlike nomad Quadi tribe. It was situated at the northwest corner of what now includes the Graben, the Tiefen Graben, Naglergasse, Rotgasse and Kraemergasse. Emperor Marcus Aurelius died here in 180 A.D. Not only had he led the war against the Marcomanni, but he had also found time and inspiration to write a good part of his Meditations. Upon his death the barbarians whom the emperor had sought to keep at bay were free to overflow the entire region. Between the 5th and 7th centuries, the Danubian plain in all its length and breadth was the theater of barbarian incursions. Ostrogoths, Vandals, Huns, Slavs, Avars poured into Pannonia in successive waves. The destiny of the region and of the city changed in 791 when Charlemagne founded the Western Empire and created the Ostmark, the Eastern March, which was to constitute the principle nucleus of Ostarrîchi, the future Österreich, or realm of the East. Wenia, the new name of the city, also appears for the first time in a document from Salzburg in 881.
The Ostmark was ceded in 976 by Emperor Otto II to Count Leopold I of the Babenberg dynasty, thus making him the first hereditary margrave in Austria. The region was now independent and the city flourished under this dynasty thanks in great part to its fortunate location on the Danube. It immediately became an important river port and a large trading center, situated as it was on the amber route. Long long ago, before the birth of Christ, merchants had already been carrying amber to the southern parts of Europe. Under Henry II called Jasomirgott (who transformed the

Austrian March into a hereditary duchy) the city rose to the rank of residence when the duke moved his court there from Klosterneuburg. The Babenberg dynasty ended with Frederick II and in 1282, after a period of anarchy and struggles, the city passed under the dominion of Rudolf I, founder of the Hapsburg family which was to rule over Austria for almost six centuries. These then were the beginnings of Vienna and as the city grew in size it grew in beauty. The Cathedral of St. Stephen already dominated the city from on high. The first University had already been founded. In 1438, under Albert V, Vienna became the capital of the Holy Roman Empire and the Hapsburg dynasty attained the imperial rank which it was to hold until 1806 when Napoleon abolished the Holy Roman Empire a thousand years after its inception. The only brief interruption occured in 1485 when Matthias Corvinus entered the city at the head of the Hungarian army and occupied it until 1490. The old fortified settlement was a thing of the past and Vienna was now a city of imperial status, subject to no one but the emperor, with a wealth of churches and a flourishing vital culture. When Maximilian I mounted the throne its splendor rose to great new heights. He began the open-minded policy of marriages aimed at acquiring new lands and privileges. His own marriage to Mary of Burgundy in 1477 added Burgundy and the Netherlands to the Empire. In 1496 his son Philip I called the Handsome married Juana called la Loca whose dowry included Castille and Aragon. At the death of the old Maximilian, his grandson Charles inherited everything and became king of Spain under the name of Charles I and emperor of the Holy Roman Empire as Charles V. What better way of realizing the famous motto «Bella gerant alii, tu, felix Austria, nube» (Others bring wars, you, happy Austria, bring weddings). Thus Vienna found itself the capital of the empire «on which the sun never set» and as such began to play an extremely important role in European history.

It became no less than the last bulwark of western civilization when the Turkish empire, ever more threatening, began to press against the gates of Europe. The Turks, to whom Constantinople had fallen in 1453, invaded Hungary in 1526 and Austria was all that remained between them and the western world. The wars against the Turks exhausted the city which was besieged twice, once in 1529 and again in 1683. Finally in 1697, thanks to Eugene Prince of Savoy, who defeated the Turks at Zenta, the danger was definitively averted. Despite Charles V's repeated attempts to realize a universal monarchy, his hegemonic dream was doomed to failure, unable to withstand the hard blows inflicted by the spread of the Reformation and by the growing affirmation of the principle of the autonomy of the individual nations. Even so Vienna was as resplendent as ever under the enlightened reign of Maria Theresa and then of her son Joseph. The city throve and rivalled even Paris for first place among European cities in the fields of art, culture, politics, and economy. This was the beginning of that «mitteleuropean» culture which was to dominate all of Europe until the end of the Hapsburg dominion. When the wars against France were finally over Vienna also became the political center of Europe, and in 1815 played host to the famous Congress which attempted to bring peace to the countries that had been lashed by the Napoleonic cyclone. Austria acted as arbiter for European political policy of which Metternich was the chief exponent and took the role of guarantor for all the sovereign states of the conservative reactionary trend which aimed at repressing the movements for liberation and autonomy of the individual populations. A final golden age for Vienna was the reign of Francis Joseph, when the city was modernized and embellished. It now really looked like an imperial city and, most extraordinary of all, the population rose from 360,000 to more than two million inhabitants, making it the largest urban center in central Europe. But the fall of the Austro-Hungarian monarchy was not far off. Despite the enlightened reign of so many monarchs, despite their patronage, above all of music which was queen of the arts for two centuries (the 18th and 19th centuries), despite the creativity of so many geniuses, the milieu in which Vienna and the empire existed was splendidly but extremely delicately balanced. The period of Francis Joseph's long reign was only apparently stable. Actually the empire was slowly crumbling away under the weight of too many different nationalities divided by contrasting interests. The tragic revolver shots fired at Sarajevo were the spark that set off the ultimate cruel tragedy of the Hapsburg Empire. The city's age of splendor came to an end. When in 1918 the Republic of Austria was proclaimed, Vienna was relegated to being nothing but the simple capital of a small country. In addition to the enormous problems that the impoverishment and misery left by the war had created, Austria now found itself suddenly deprived of the many ethnic groups (Czechs, Poles, Croatians, Slovenes, Magyars) which had up to then been subject to the Hapsburgs. But the identity crisis through which the country was passing had not yet reached its nadir. In 1938 Austria and Vienna met their inevitable fate. Incorporated into the German Third Reich, Vienna hoped for a moment to relive its imperial role once more but it was soon clear that the supremacy of Berlin did not allow for decentralization of this sort and so the city also lost its role as capital of a federal state. Occupied by the Russians in April, 1945, it was subject to a quadripartite Allied administration. Although it was less severe than that of Germany, the allied occupation of Austria lasted ten long years. During this period, with Renner and Korner as presidents, thanks to the contribution of politically middle-of-the-road and moderate currents the country succeeded in laying a solid foundation for its reconstruction. When the occupation came to an end in 1955, Vienna was once more the theater for the signing of a treaty. On May 15, in the Palace of the Upper Belvedere, the agreement was ratified which restored full sovereignty to Austria, averting any claims the Hapsburgs might still have and guaranteeing perpetual neutrality. The city, which had already repaired a good part of the war damages, was now able to look at its future, at its problems, with renewed hope. No longer an imperial capital, but an equidistant pole of attraction, with solid economic foundations and an efficient administration, Vienna has once more regained the serenity and gracious living for which it is famous throughout the world.

We have divided the whole framework of the artistic, cultural, historic and shopping attractions offered by Vienna into eight different itineraries.

Each suggested route leads tourists across Vienna's most characteristic areas, pointing out not only monuments, churches, museums and the most famous buildings, but also points of interest, and peculiarities of the city.

For more hasty visitors, the absolute «musts» are printed in boldface.

I
p. 12 **St. Stephen's Cathedral** – St. Stephen's Square – **Graben** – **Am Hof** – Uhrenmuseum (Clock Museum) – **Freyung** – Schottenkirche – Freyung-Passage.

II
p. 24 Michaelerplatz – **Hofburg** – Michaelertrakt – **Kaiserappartements** (Imperial Apartments) – **«In der Burg»** – Amalienburg – Leopoldinischer-trakt – Reichskanzleitrakt – Alte Burg – Burgkapelle (Imperial Chapel) – **Weltliche und Geistliche Schatzkammer** (Secular and Religious Treasury) – Heldenplatz – Neue Burg – The Museums of the Neue Burg – The Hofburg Gardens – Stallburg – Josefsplatz – Nationalbibliothek (National Library) – **Spanische Hofreitschule** (Spanish Riding School) – Augustinerkirche (Church of the Augustinians) – Albertina.

III
p. 40 **Staatsoper** – Hotel Sacher – **Kärntnerstrasse** – **Kaisergruft** – Stadtpalais des Prinzen Eugen (Winter Palace of Prince Eugene) – Franziskanerkirche (Franciscan Church) – Figarohaus – Dominikanerkirche (Dominican Church) – Schönlaterngasse – Heiligenkreuzerhof – Bernhardkapelle (Chapel of St. Bernard) – Jesuitenkirche (Jesuit Church) – Akademie der Wissenschaften (Academy of Sciences) – Alte Universität (Old University) – **Hoher Markt** – **Altes Rathaus** – Bömische Hofkanzlei – Judenplatz – **Maria am Gestade** (Church of St. Mary on the Banks) – Fleischmarkt – **Ruprechtskirche** (Church of St. Rupert).

7

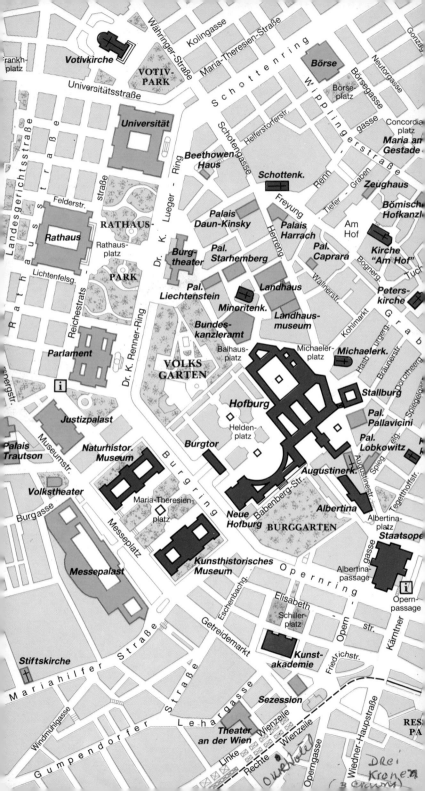

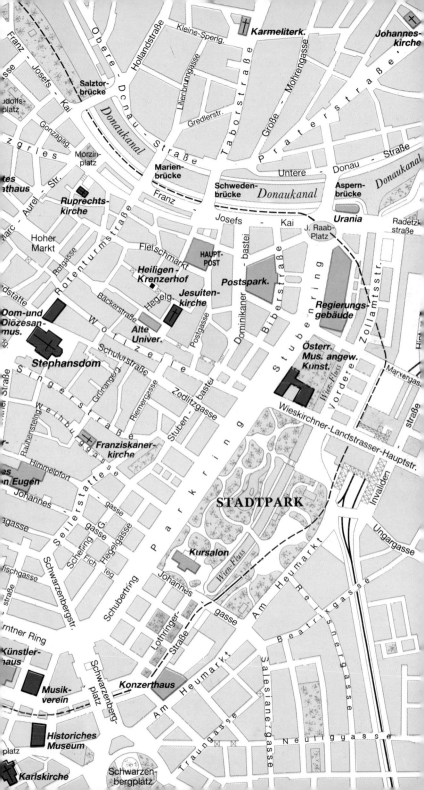

ST. STEPHEN'S CATHEDRAL

In 1263, in the brief interregnum between the Babenbergs and the Hapsburgs, construction of the first church in Romanesque style was finished under Ottokar II of Bohemia. In 1369, above all at the instigation of Duke Rudolf IV, work was begun on enlarging the church and transforming it in Gothic style. The choir and the nave were built and the south tower, which was to be finished in 1433, was begun.

At the time of Emperor Frederick III, in 1469, Vienna became an

Main entrance portal of the Cathedral.

episcopal see and the construction of the north tower, which was never finished, was begun. The polychrome roof of 1490 was done under Matthias I Corvinus who briefly ruled the city.

In the 1700s the furnishings in baroque style appeared but the structure of the church remained unchanged.

In the last days of the second world war, in April of 1945, the building was heavily bombed and fire broke out. Long and careful restoration financed with the help of all the Austrian Länder and finished in 1956 has restored the church, pride and symbol of the whole nation, to its original splendor.

The cathedral is 107 meters long and 38.9 meters high at the nave. The massive compact bulk is lightened and enriched by the towers and spires which surround it and by the steeply pitched roof covered with colored tiles. Once supported on larch rafters, the roof was completely destroyed in 1945 and has since been rebuilt with steel beams.

FACADE – The main entrance and the two massive towers on either side, known as **Heathens' Towers**, are all that remain of the first Romanesque building. Of particular note is the portal, the **Riesentor**, or Giant's Doorway, decorated with geometric figures, zoomorphic motifs and sacred images. Particularly interesting are the small figures of the *stone mason* in the left-hand corner and a *St. Peter* with an enormous key. In the tympanum a seated *Christ* with a book in one hand and with his left knee uncovered is flanked by two angels. This relief has been the subject of endless discussion among art historians, some of whom have interpreted it as a reference to Masonic rites which obliged neophytes to present themselves at the initiation ceremony with their left knee uncovered. Other Romanesque sculptures on the facade include a griffin and *Samson and the lion* to the right of the door.

The external façade bears the 05 symbol of the Austrian resistance against the Nazis and «Anschluss» with Hitler's Germany. Number 5 stands for the fifth letter of the alphabet: 05 = OE = Oesterreich.

EXTERIOR – Proceeding along the right (south) side of the cathedral one comes to the **Singertor** or Singers' Doorway by master Puchsbaum, with a Gothic portal of 1450 which is decorated with many statues and bas-reliefs and rivals the main portal in beauty. In a niche on the left side is a *statue of Rudolf IV* holding a model of the first Romanesque church.

Continuing along the side, we come to the baroque lower sacris-

Exterior of the Cathedral: on the left, the statue of Rudolf IV;
on the right, the high relief above the Capistrano pulpit.

14

ty, and shooting up to the sky like an arrow, the tall profile of the south tower, **Steffl** or little Stephen as it is familiarly called by the Viennese. Decorated with pinnacles and spires and 136 meters high, it is one of the masterpieces of the Gothic and without doubt the finest bell tower in Vienna. The unique shape of a square base which becomes octagonal near the top helps give the tower its lithe elegant aspect. Inside, a narrow spiral staircase with 343 steps leads to the «tower room» with a splendid view of the city.

Continuing around the outside of the church towards the apse, one encounters 16th-century reliefs, statues and a 15th-century pulpit known as the **Capistrano Pulpit** because in 1451 St. John of Capistrano preached a crusade against the Turks from here. Particularly noteworthy is the 15th-century statue of *Our Lord with a Toothache* (the one outside is a copy of the original which is inside on the side of the north tower), which tradition would have the gift of a sinner who was cured and redeemed.

Lastly, on the north side of the cathedral, the north tower known as **Adlerturm** (Eagle Tower), 60 meters high and with a Renaissance steeple finished in 1578 by the architects Kaspar and Saphai. Inside the tower is one of the largest bells extant, the *Pummerin* (or Boomer), more than 21,000 kilograms of bronze which were cast in 1717 from captured Turkish cannons. After its destruction during the last war, it was recast. Here too one can ascend to the belvedere (but this time using the comfortable elevator inside the church) to admire the bell and the city.

INTERIOR – Striking in its imposing graceful structure with a nave and two aisles of equal height and length, and for the wealth of its decoration, this fusion of Gothic and baroque creates a uniquely beautiful whole.

The light that enters through the large windows (most of the original stained glass was destroyed in 1945) illuminates the daring design of the ribs which lead from the columns to the vaulted ceiling.

Let us begin our visit with the right aisle. The 14th-century *statue of the Virgin Mary* in the **Ducal Chapel** or **Chapel of St. Eligius** is worthy of note. A bit further on, under a baldachin of 1510, illuminated by hundreds of candles offered in devotion by the Viennese, is a 17th-century icon known as the *Madonna of the Tears*, decorated in gold and and silver and originally from the Hungarian town of Pötsch. Almost at the level of the transept is the entrace to the **lower sacristy**, a baroque construction added in the 1700s. The frescoes in the ceiling are by Altomonte.

Some of St. Stephen's finest treasures are to be found in the nave. Particular attention should be paid, at the level of the third column on the left, to the **Pulpit** by Anton Pilgram, a Gothic masterpiece executed in 1510 and perhaps the loveliest of all. The unbelievable openwork of the parapet and the base, the mysterious thoughtful faces of the four *Fathers of the Church* (Augustine, Gregory, Jerome, Ambrose), the wealth of details, all result in a harmonious unique structure. An oddity and a masterpiece within the masterpiece is Pilgram's «signature» in the base of the

St. Stephen's Cathedral: interior.

work, a *self-portrait* in which the artist represented himself as if he were peering out of a half-open window.

In addition to the numerous baroque altars built against the pillars, the nave contains the 14th-century *Madonna of the Servants*, to be seen near the pulpit. It is the legendary bequest of an aristocratic lady who had unjustly accused her maid of theft.

At the beginning of the left aisle, fenced off by a baroque iron railing, is the **Kreuzkapelle** (or Tirna Chapel) with the *tomb of Prince Eugene of Savoy*, who defeated the Turks in the 17th century. The coats of arms of the house of Savoy and of Liechtenstein decorate the railings. Next to the chapel is a fine *Gothic baldachin of the 15th century*, attributed to H. von Prachatitz. Almost at the end of the aisle is another work by Pilgram: the organ support

(1513) which in this case too is «signed» by the master who portrayed himself holding a compass and a T-square. The organ was removed some time ago and the organ loft was transformed into a singers' gallery.

In the left transept is the **Crypt**, a simple structure dating back to 1752 which leads to the catacombs that have housed the remains of the archbishops of Vienna since 1953. Rudolf IV had already had a crypt built there in 1363 for the Hapsburgian dukes. Maria Theresa had it enlarged in 1754 and since then it has been the home for the copper urns containing the royal family's viscera while their embalmed corpses are found in the Kapuzinerkirche and their hearts in the Augustinerkirche. In the catacombs, the *tomb of Rudolf*, founder of the Hapsburg dynasty, can be seen.

The choir is also divided into three aisles with apses. On the right is the **Choir of the Apostles** with the *tomb in red marble of Frederick III*. This impressive mausoleum decorated with hundreds of figures, coats of arms and reliefs was begun by Nikolaus Gerhaert von Leyden in 1467 and finished 46 years later.

In the central apse a large canvas representing the *Lapidation of St. Stephen* hangs over the **high altar** in baroque style by Tobias Pock (1667).

Finally, on the left, the **Women's Choir**, with a carved and painted Gothic altarpiece of 1447, with scenes from the life of the Virgin, originally from the Cistercian monastery of Wiener Neustadt. Near the altar is the *cenotaph of Duke Rudolf IV*.

Detail of the interior: on the left, pulpit by Anton Pilgram; on the right, Gothic altarpiece in the Women's Choir.

A room in the Cathedral and Diocesan Museum.

ST. STEPHEN'S SQUARE

Stephansplatz is a large 18th-century square surrounding the imposing bulk of the cathedral and is greatly ehanced by the fact that it has recently been closed to traffic.

Upon leaving the church, as soon as one is outside the main portal the first thing to do is descend into the modern underground station and take a look at the remains of the **Virgilkapelle** (Chapel of St. Virgil). This authentic 13th-century crypt is situated in the cemetery which surrounded the cathedral up to 1783 and which was brought to light when the subway was built. Near the chapel one can see a small collection of pottery and other archaeological material which turned up during the excavation.

To the left of the facade the square turns into a delightful parking place for the «fiaker», the picturesque horse cabs available (for a fee) to anyone who wants to take a romantic spin around the city. Continuing around the cathedral one encounters noteworthy buildings such as the **Churhaus** (Nursing Home) at n. 3 built between 1738 and 1740, the **Domherren Hof** (Rectory) and at n. 6 the **Dom- und Diözesanmuseum** (Cathedral and Diocesan Museum) which houses an important collection of religious art and early medieval objects from the Treasury of St. Stephen's, together with painted Gothic panels, sculpture and examples of baroque and Romantic art. Of particular note in Room 1, the *Portrait of Duke Rudolf IV*, probably painted in 1365 by H. Vaschang; Room 3: Gothic sculpture and painting and a fine 14th-century stained glass window; in Room 4 is an *Ecce Homo* by Cranach the Elder.

Almost on the same level as «Steffl» but with an entrance in the adjacent Singerstrasse, at n. 7, is the **Kirche und Schatzkammer des Deutschen Ordens**, the church and treasury of the ancient Order of the Teutonic Knights. The church, built in 1375, is one of the few Gothic buildings that was not radically remodelled in baroque style. Of particular interest is the 16th-century Dutch *triptych* which was kept in the Church of St. Mary in Danzig until 1864. The **Treasury** also merits a visit: crockery and precious furnishings of the 17th and 18th centuries as well as insignia, coins, ceremonial outfits and weapons comprise the treasure of this medieval order of knights which originated in Germany and became very powerful before it had to emigrate to Vienna in an attempt to escape persecution on the part of Napoleon who considered it a dangerous obstacle to his project of dominion over the German nation.

18

GRABEN

Together with Kärntnerstrasse and Kohlmarkt the Graben forms the business center of Vienna where one goes for shopping, for appointments and for casual encounters.

A pedestrian area, the Graben has a unique shape – it is in fact an elongated plaza, 300 meters long and over 30 meters wide. It is on the site of a ditch which was part of the defenses of the Roman encampment (in German Graben means ditch) and which was filled in 1255 and transformed into an open space for the food market and surrounded by buildings. In Maria Theresa's time the Graben became famous as the meeting place of Viennese aristocracy, as well as the favorite haunt of prostitutes, frequented by the no less famous «Ninfe del Graben».

The baroque **Pestsäule** (Plague Column or Trinity Column) dominates the center of the square. It was erected as thanks for the end of the plague of 1679 by J. B. Fischer von Erlach and Ludovico Ottavio Burnacini, with the collaboration of other well-known artists of the time. Two 19th-century fountains, symmetrically set at either end of the square, complete the decoration. Various

Two views of the Graben: on the left, the baroque Pestsäule (Plague Column); on the right, the 18th-century Church of St. Peter.

19th-century buildings are also of interest, including the **Sparkasse** (former Savings Bank) at n. 21, in Biedermeier style, and the Art Nouveau buildings at n. 10, n. 14-15 and n. 16, the latter decorated at the top with colored tiles. On the right of the Graben, coming from the cathedral, is a square with the **Peterskirche** (St. Peter's Church), remodelled by J.L. von Hildebrandt in baroque style in 1703, on the site of a precedent church supposedly dating back to Charlemagne. The **interior**, lavishly decorated with gold and ocher stuccoes and numerous frescoes, was the work of the most talented baroque artists including M. Altomonte, L. Mattielli, M. Steinl, S. Bussi and A. Camesina. The *fresco in the dome* is a masterpiece by J.M. Rottmayr.

AM HOF

Lovely elegant Naglergasse, now a pedestrian zone, leads directly to the heart of the ancient city, Am Hof.
This large square of an almost trapezoidal form has been the center of the political and social life of the city for centuries and is still one of the most significant squares of the Innere Stadt. It was here that the Romans had their encampment of Vindobona. It was here that the Babenbergs built their palace in the 12th century (which is why it is called Am Hof, or at the court). It was here, for centuries, that tournaments and spectacles were organized for the sovereigns. Now various fine buildings and a church stand around a typically Viennese square.
At the center is the **Mariensäule** (Column of the Virgin). Set up in 1667 to replace another column of 1646, it was the work of B. Herold, C.M. Carlone and C. Canevale. At its base four figures symbolize what the city feared most: *war, famine, plague, heresy.*
The **Kirche am Hof** or Church of the Nine Angelic Choirs, built around 1400 by the Carmelites, was destroyed by fire and rebuilt in baroque style in 1610. The Italian architect C.A. Carlone designed the facade of 1662, a fine example of early baroque. The **interior** has a nave and two aisles with a choir. Frescoes and stuccoes decorate the walls, the side chapels and the dome. The large painting on the high altar is by G.J. Daringer. It was from the terrace on the rear facade, that Pope Pious VI blessed the Viennese in 1782 and it was from this same terrace that the announcement was made on August 6, 1806, of Francis II's renunciation of the crown of the Holy Roman Empire, after Napoleon's troops had «convinced» him to end this centuries-old political entity.

Next to the church, at n. 13, is **Palais Collalto** where the child Mozart gave his first concert. At one corner of the square is the firemen's barracks, which occupy the old **Bürgerliche Zeughaus** (City Arsenal), an ostentatious 16th-century building decorated on the facade with statues by Lorenzo Mattielli.

**View of the Kirche am Hof
on the square of the same name.**

In one of the alleys behind the church, at Schulhof n. 2, the **Uhrenmuseum** (Clock Museum), one of the most interesting and strange museums in the city, can be visited. This old building, with its simple entrance, contains 3000 clocks that span a period of four centuries and are true masterpieces of mechanical art. Truly admirable for their richness are the watches decorated with inlays of ivory, enamels, silver and semi-precious stones. Meanwhile, for a touch of the bizarre, there is amongst others, a hand-made clock of rural origin, with a pendulum in the form of a cow's tail. The astronomical clock, whose hands make a full turn once every 20.904 years, the tiny pocket watches and the hundreds of mechanisms which combine skill, precision and imagination make this museum a must.

FREYUNG

A short street connects Am Hof to Freyung, another large square in old Vienna, of irregular form, dominated by the Schottenkirche (Church of the Scots) and surrounded by numerous fine buildings. The name of the square comes from the German «frei» or free, because in the Middle Ages wayfarers and the persecuted could take advantage of the right of asylum granted to the Scottish church by the sovereign.

Palais Daun-Kinsky,
a fine example of Austrian baroque.

For centuries it was known as an infamous place, where drop-outs and all sorts of strange individuals met.

Today a walk around the square reveals other art treasures – at n. 3 is the **Harrach Palais**, built around 1690 probably on designs by Domenico Martinelli; at n. 4 is the **Palais Daun-Kinsky**, one of the loveliest buildings of the Austrian baroque created between 1713 and 1716 by J. Lukas von Hildebrandt (take special note of the *great staircase* inside); at n. 7 is the **House of the cupboard with drawers**, an odd but fitting name for the 18th-century Priory of the Monastery of the Scots, which does indeed look just like a chest of drawers. At the center of the square is the **Austria-Brunnen** (Austria Fountain), with allegoric statues of the four rivers of the Hapsburg empire (Po, Vistola, Elbe, Danube), erected in 1846.

SCHOTTENKIRCHE – The church dates back to the 12th century when the first of the Babenbergs to reside in Vienna, Duke Henry II Jasomirgott, made conspicuous donations to a group of Benedictine monks of Irish origin – erroneously called Scottish – who built a Romanesque church on this site. In the centuries that followed fires and various vicissitudes destroyed the complex which was reconstructed more than once until finally Andrea Felice d'Allio and Silvestro Carlone gave it its present baroque aspect between 1643 and 1648. It was further modified in the 19th century.

The simple facade is flanked by two low massive towers. Of note **inside** are the baroque side altars, the ceiling **paintings** by Julius Schmid and the *high altar*, a more recent work of 1883 by H. von Ferstel. On the left is the entrance to the *monumental crypt* where Duke Henry is buried.

FREYUNG-PASSAGE – A real hidden treasure is this gallery between Freyung and Herrengasse, which was created in the middle of the 19th century as the headquarters for the stock exchange agencies and which was then almost abandoned until recent radical restoration restored the complex to its original splendor, in Biedermeier style, by the architect H. von Ferstel. Corridors, courtyards, flights of stairs covered by glass vaulting, delicately colored marble, and the splendid small square with the **Fountain of the Danubian Nymphs** provide ideal surroundings in which to visit the large elegant shops which now occupy Freyung-passage. At this point it might be a good idea to stop for a while at the Café Central, a favorite meeting place of Viennese intellectuals in the last decades of the monarchy and now perfectly restored.

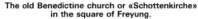

The old Benedictine church or «Schottenkirche» in the square of Freyung.

MICHAELERPLATZ

This lovely plaza, of a vaguely triangular form, is the starting point for anyone who wants to get to the heart of imperial Vienna. Here the statues and fountains of the Michaelertrakt (see p. 27) herald the main entrance to the royal residence of the Hapsburgs, focal point of the hopes and grudges of 50,000,000 subjects.

Michaelerplatz with its wealth of art works merits more than just a hurried visit.

Michaelerkirche with its picturesque spire.

The **Michaelerkirche** (St. Michael's Church) draws the attention of the visitor at first sight. It was initially built in the first half of the 13th century in a late Romanesque style and was later transformed and enlarged in Gothic, baroque and neoclassic styles. The neoclassic facade by E. Koch (1793) is simple and austere, preceded by a baroque portico decorated with a sculpture group of the archangel Michael by L. Mattielli. Towering over it is the spire of the Gothic bell tower built in 1598. The interior has a nave and two aisles with a choir and a transept. The high altar (1781) is the last example of baroque art in Vienna. Over the altar is a 16th-century *Byzantine icon* from Crete. The *Tomb of the poet Pietro Metastasio* is in the left transept. In the right transept is a large 18th-century canvas by M. Unterberger of the *Fall of the Rebel Angels.*

Opposite St. Michael's, in sharp contrast to the decorations and tinsel of the imperial palace, is the sober unadorned facade of **Looshaus**, built in 1910 by the great architect Adolf Loos, one of the principal exponents of the Viennese Art Nouveau. His building is no other than a protest against the so-called «Ringstrasse style» with its craze for ostentation, its imitations, its overabundant decoration. The protest hit the mark, and engendered the wrath of emperor Francis Joseph, who complained of that «horrible house without eyebrows» which lay right across from his window. The **Kohlmarkt**, a rich and lively business street which leads to the Graben, also opens off Michaelerplatz. At n. 11 is the famous café-pastry shop «Demel», the temple of Viennese gastronomy.

HOFBURG

For seven centuries the Hofburg was the palace of the Hapsburgs who reigned here first as emperors of the Holy Roman Empire and then, after 1806, as emperors of Austria. Continuously

The facade of the Hofburg on Michaelerplatz.

The fountains on either side of the Hofburg:
on the left, «Austria's Dominion over the Sea»;
on the right, «Austria's Dominion over the Earth».

enlarged and transformed over the years, the complex of 18 buildings, 19 courtyards, 54 staircases, 2600 rooms, lacks an architectural and stylistic unity. This historical-artistic «compendium» of the Hapsburg monarchy testifies to the centuries of history in which each period has left a mark in some part of this strange and monumental castle. Pacts of alliance and declarations of war alternated with fabulous princely balls. Political intrigues and tender love stories lived side by side within these walls which in the course of 700 years have withstood revolutions, fires and six sieges. Still today the Hofburg plays an important part in Austrian and in international political life, housing the most important governmental bodies of the country and an important center for congresses.

MICHAELERTRAKT – Built in 1883 on an earlier design by the great baroque architect J. E. Fischer von Erlach on the site of the first seat of the «National and Court Theater», St. Michael's wing became the main entrance to the castle. A large hemicycle covered by a dome leads from Michaelerplatz into the vast courtyard known as «**In der Burg**». The facade is decorated with statues and flanked by two fountains which celebrate the power of the Hapsburgs on land and sea: on the right *Austria's Dominion over* *the Earth*, of 1897, on the left, *Austria's Dominion over the Sea*, of 1895.

Once inside the main entrance, on the left (coming from Michaelerplatz) is the entrance to the State apartments.

KAISERAPPARTAMENTS – A visit not to be missed. The imperial apartments open to the public (guided visit) are all in the wing of the Imperial Chancellery and in the Amalienburg.

Wandering through these rooms is an unforgettable experience. You will discover the aristocratic simplicity of Emperor Francis Joseph, or the meticulous care his lovely wife Elizabeth lavished on her body, with baths, beauty masks and exercises; or you can admire the delicate rococo decorations of the rooms where Czar Alexander I was guest during the Congress of Vienna (1815), the lovely Louis XV or Empire furniture and the chandeliers in Bohemian crystal, and you will marvel at the table laid for a meal in the dining room.

The visit begins with the **Apartment of Archduke Stephen**, composed of four rooms which contain 17th-century *Brussels tapestries*. Next come the **Apartment of Francis Joseph** (including the Biedermeier fete hall, with *murals* by Peter Kraft, and the Council Room); the **Apartment of Elizabeth** (composed of four rooms, in addition to the bedroom and the dressing room; noteworthy the *statue of Elisa Bonaparte* by Antonio Canova, of 1817); the **Apartment of Alexander** (composed of six rooms, decorated with 17th- and 18th-century *tapestries* from Paris and Brussels); and the **imperial dining room** which concludes the series of rooms that can be visited.

Hofburg: the sumptuous elegance of the «Red Room» decorated with Gobelin tapestries.

The opposite side of the rotonda of St. Michael's leads to the **Hoftafel- und Silberkammer** with dinner services and silverware used at court banquets including a fine collection of *Chinese and Japanese 18th-century porcelain, sets of Sèvres china*, a set of dishes for 140 persons in enamel decorated in vermeil, a 19th-century bronze centerpiece 30 meters long, and other crockery.

«IN DER BURG» – Upon leaving the rotonda of St. Michael's wing one enters this spacious internal courtyard which was created in 1545 as a tournament field for Archduke Maximilian. If the Swiss Court (see page 31) is the expression of the Gothic period and Heldenplatz (see page 34) that of the 19th century, the «Platz in der Burg» is where baroque art has left its deepest and most lasting mark. Used for tournaments and royal fetes (particularly to be remembered is the reception of 1660 on the occa-

The Imperial dining room
with the table set for a «family meal».

28

Franz Winterhalter: Emperor Francis Joseph
and Empress Elizabeth (1865).

sion of the wedding of Leopold I with Margaret of Spain), this
courtyard was also the scene of dramatic events such as the exe-
cution of numerous officers and soldiers who had betrayed their
country during the war against the Turks. At the center of the
square is the *monument to Emperor Francis I* who died in 1835.
At present the square provides access to the Amalienburg, the
Leopoldine wing, Heldenplatz, the wing of the Imperial Chancellery and, through the magnificent Swiss Portal, to the Swiss
Courtyard.

AMALIENBURG – This wing was built between 1575 and
1611 at the request of Emperor Rudolf II.
During Maria Theresa's reign the interior decoration was completely renovated. Noteworthy is the **Tower**, built in 1764 by N.
Pacassi, with an *astronomical clock* that indicates the phases of
the moon, the work of the great court astronomer at the time of
Rudolf II, Tycho de Brahe.
The empress Amalia, widow of Joseph I, lived here from 1711
until 1742, the year she died. The building is named after her.

LEOPOLDINISCHERTRAKT – The construction of the Leopoldine wing, which unites the Swiss Courtyard to the Amalienburg was begun in the 16th century, in 1547. A fire destroyed a good
part of the building and it was practically rebuilt by Ludovico
Burnacini between 1660 and 1668. This was when the baroque
transformation of the imperial residence began. Empress Maria
Theresa and her husband Francis Stephen of Lorraine lived in this
wing of the palace which still contains the furniture chosen by the

29

Hofburg. Above: the monument to Emperor Francis I;
below: the Renaissance portal in the
Schweizerhof (Swiss Court).

empress. In 1946 it became the official seat of the president of the Federal Republic of Austria, whose presence is announced by the Austrian flag flying outside the building.

REICHSKANZLEITRAKT – Lukas von Hildebrandt and Joseph Emanuel Fischer von Erlach, the two great architects of the Austrian baroque, designed the monumental north wing (wing of the Imperial Chancellery) begun in 1723 and finished in 1730. Lorenzo Mattielli sculptured the *Labors of Hercules* which decorate the main entrance. Up to 1806 the offices of the Holy Roman Empire had their headquarters here.

ALTE BURG – In a document of King Rudolf I of Germany dated February 14, 1279 mention is made of this simple fortified castle erected a few years earlier by the Bohemian king Ottokar II who ruled briefly over Vienna.

All that is left of the original construction, square in plan with four massive towers at the corners, is the so-called **Schweizerhof** (Swiss Court), so fully modified in the 15th and 16th centuries as to lose its medieval aspect. The name of the courtyard, like that of the **Schweizertor**, a fine Renaissance portal of 1552, brick red with gold inscriptions (on the site of the drawbridge of the first castle), derives from the Swiss guards who had their barracks in this part of the building.

Schatzkammer: the crown of the Holy Roman Empire set with precious stones and enamel. It was made in 962 for the coronation of Otto I.

The entrance to the **Burgkapelle** (or Imperial Chapel), perhaps the oldest part of the Hofburg, is in the courtyard. The present building was erected in 1449 in the reign of Frederick III on the site of a chapel built in 1296 for Duke Albert I. Nikolaus Gerhaert von Leyden was probably the architect who designed the church, and the *13 wooden statues of Saints* inside are surely by his hand. The baroque additions date to the time of Maria Theresa. A marble tabernacle contains *Ferdinand's cross*, a masterpiece of 16th-century Spanish wood sculpture. Its name derives from the fact that when Emperor Ferdinand was involved in the religious wars against the Protestants he was miraculously encouraged in his struggles by a voice as he was praying in front of the cross.

Sunday morning one can listen to the splendid concerts of the Vienna Boys' Choir accompanied by the musicians of the Vienna Philharmonic.

Entrance to the **Weltliche und Geistliche Schatzkammer** (Secular and Religious Treasury) is also from the Swiss Court. This is one of the most interesting collections of precious objects and historical-religious relics in the world. Hundreds of items of inestimable value testify to the complex vicissitudes of the Holy Roman Empire and its deep ties with the Catholic church and the Catholic religion.

The museum is divided into two parts: 11 rooms contain the «Secular Treasure» including the insignia of the Holy Roman Empire (*imperial crown* of 962; *imperial orb* of the 12th century; *silver scepter*, 14th century; *imperial robe*, of the 12th century, (woven in Palermo of Chinese silk for King Roger II); the *imperial crown of the Hapsburgs* of 1602; a *basin* and a *pitcher* in solid gold used for imperial christenings; the *silver cradle*, weighing all of 280 kilograms, donated to Napoleon I by the city of Paris for his son, the king of Rome.

Special mention must be made of the «Treasure of the Knights of the Golden Fleece or the Treasure of Burgundy» which became part of the Hapsburg property when through marriage they

The impressive Heldenplatz, once the stage
for the review of the imperial army.

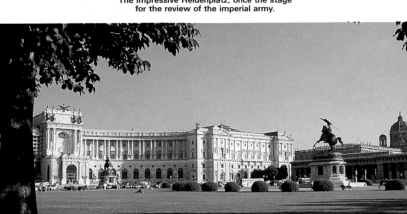

Heldenplatz: equestrian monuments dedicated to Archduke
Charles (left) and Prince Eugene of Savoy (right).

added the title of dukes of Burgundy to the ones they already
had. Outstanding among the many valuable objects are the
priests' vestments of the 15th century, considered masterpieces of medieval art, and a *Flemish collar* of 1517 in gold and enamel. Six other rooms contain the «Religious Treasure» which com-
prises *reliquaries, religious vestments, statues* and representa-
tions of religious subjects. After considerable restoration, the
treasury is once again open to visitors.

HELDENPLATZ – After returning to the square «In der Burg»,
an underpassage in the Leopoldine wing leads to the vast Square
of the Heroes, a large open space used for parades of the imperial army, dominated by the *statues of Archduke Charles and
Prince Eugene of Savoy*. To the left of the square the Neue Burg
opens in a semi-circle, and on the side opposite the Leopoldine
wing is the Burgtor (see page 51) while the Volksgarten borders
on the right-hand side of the square.

NEUE BURG – This colossal building was the last expression of
Hapsburg power. Finished in 1913, it was supposed to be the
first part of a grandiose «imperial forum» designed by G. Semper.
The Austro-Hungarian defeat of 1918 put an end to the empire
and its dreams of glory. The wing of the palace which connects
it to the Leopoldine wing contains an enormous banquet hall of
over 1,000 square meters, now seat of the Congress Center.
Part of the National Library and numerous museums are inside
the Neue Burg (literally New Castle).

Neue Burg: two suits of armor from
the Arms Collection.

THE MUSEUMS OF THE NEUE BURG – The imperial palace
also houses a large number of collections and museums. Some
have already been mentioned. Some of the others will be mentioned in the following pages.

Ephesos Museum – At the beginning of the century and right after World War II
Austrian archaeologists carried out extensive excavations in Asia Minor, particularly around Ephesos. The results of these excavations are now preserved in this museum, called Ephesos Museum, organized according to the most modern museum
criteria. The large *bas-relief* of the 2nd century, over 70 meters long, in memory
of the victory of Lucius Verus and Marcus Aurelius over the Parthians (165), the *octagonal tomb* of a young woman, and part of the *sacrificial altar* from the great temple of Artemis are to be noted.

The same ticket also admits one to the **Collection of weapons** of the 14th to the
19th centuries, and to the **Collection of antique musical instruments**, with its
harpsichords, pianos and other instruments that belonged to the great names of
Austrian music.

The **Museum für Völkerkunde** (or Ethnological Museum) contains objects from
all parts of the world, including, on the ground floor, bronzes from the kingdom of
Benin in Africa (from 1100 to 1800), the famous *feather crown* and the *shield* decorated with plumes and turquoises, given to Cortes by the Aztec emperor Montezuma in sign of friendship. On the first floor are also arts and crafts from Brasil, New
Guinea and Australia.

34

THE HOFBURG GARDENS – Halls, staircases, courtyards, museums – the visit to the imperial palace is a real ordeal for the tourist. Often the only thing to do is find some restful corner, a spot in which to pause and take a breather before continuing the delightful but exhausting itinerary. Nothing better then than to take advantage of those small masterpieces of tranquillity, measured beauty and harmony embodied in the two parks of the Hofburg, the **Volksgarten** (People's garden) and the **Burggarten** (Palace garden).

The former is situated at the back of Heldenplatz, the latter behind the Neue Burg. These green oases offer any number of places to rest, around fountains or the many statues, near beds of roses or under large horse chestnuts. In the Volksgarten be careful not to miss the small but charming niche dedicated to the empress Elizabeth, the romantic memoir of a greatly beloved woman, where many young Viennese couples often rendezvous. And in the Burggarten stop in front of the *statue dedicated to Mozart*, by the pool, or near the *Art Nouveau greenhouse*, just long enough to get the feel of the sweet romantic atmosphere of Vienna.

A visit to the Hofburg complex, which grew haphazardly throughout the centuries, adding a building here, another there, means turning back more than once. Even then one has to cross the square «In der Burg» again and exit through the main entrance into St. Michael's square, to get to another beautiful wing of the palace on the right.

STALLBURG – This may well be the most beautiful Renaissance building in Vienna. Originally separated from the rest of the royal palace and with a large square court surrounded by splendid porticoes, Ferdinand I had this building constructed for his son Maximilian. It was afterwards transformed into stables for the emperor's horses. The magnificent Lipizzaner horses of the Spanish Riding School are still stabled here. On the second floor of the building is the Neue Gallerie (New Gallery).

The Hofburg Gardens. Left, the monument to Empress Elizabeth in the Volksgarten; right, the monument to Mozart in the Burggarten.

Josefsplatz with the equestrian statue
of Joseph II at the center.

Neue Gallerie in der Stallburg – A rich and interesting picture gallery of modern and contemporary art, with works by Goya (Room 2), Rodin (Room 3), Toulouse-Lautrec (Room 4), Renoir, Monet, Pisarro, Degas, Manet (Room 5), Cézanne, Van Gogh, Picasso, Segantini (Room 10).

JOSEFSPLATZ – Austrian 18th-century art attains high artistic and architectonic merit in this square which is considered one of the loveliest and most harmonious squares in Vienna. Surrounded on all sides by splendid palaces, this area, which began to be used as grounds for the Riding School in 1565, took on its present form under Emperor Joseph II, who is immortalized in the *equestrian statue* in the center of the square, by the sculptor Franz Anton Zauner, of 1807. Facing the National Library, which shuts off one side of the square, the building on the right is the **Redoutensaal** (Rout Hall) of 1767, previously used as a ball room and for theatrical performances; to the left is a wing of the Augustinian Convent and on the opposite side of the library are the beautiful **Pallavicini** and **Palffy Palaces** (1784 and 1575).

Nationalbibliothek – Once more the names of the two architects Fischer von Erlach, father and son, are tied to the realization of this building, the National Library, dating to 1737. The most prestigious part is without doubt the *grand hall* frescoed by Daniel Gran. The library owns more than two million volumes as well as a thousand manuscripts, papyri, maps and photographs. Inside, exhibition rooms open to the public contain some of the library's rarest and most valuable exemplars.

SPANISCHE HOFREITSCHULE – Milk-white horses, austere and impeccable riders move against the background of a princely hall, an exhibition in which strength, skill and delicacy are impeccably and uniquely fused. All this is the famous Spanish Riding School, an institution which is more than 400 years old and which is one of the treasures of the imperial palace and of Vienna.

Although it is necessary to book months in advance if one wants to attend the performances, it is easier to observe the morning training sessions which are held daily from February to June and from September to December (except Sundays and Mondays). Waiting in line for a while is well worth the chance to see this unique spectacle in which the white Lipizzaner horses perform miracles of skill and choreographical ballets which will take your breath away. These exercises, done with such apparent ease, require years of training and a symbiosis between the rider and the horse that is difficult to attain.

**An acrobatic exercise
of the Spanische Hofreitschule.**

The school was created in 1572 for military reasons, with horses of Spanish stock which are now raised in Austria, to be trained as front-line cavalry mounts. Housed in the **Winterreitschule**, built under the direction of J.E. Fischer von Erlach between 1729 and 1735, the heart of the building is naturally the gallery where the horses go through their paces. All white and flooded with light, the 55-meter long hall is surrounded by a portico of 46 columns which support the balcony. During the Congress of Vienna sumptuous fetes were held here, like the one of October 2, 1812, in which 10,000 people took part. It was also the scene of important political events, such as the assembly of citizens during the revolution of 1848. A spacious courtyard, the Summer Riding School, opens off the back of the building.

From Josefsplatz, the Augustinerstrasse leads to the last two stages of the visit to the imperial castle, the Church of the Augustinians and the Albertina Museum.

AUGUSTINERKIRCHE – Formerly the court parish church where royal weddings were celebrated, the 14th-century Church of the Augustinians was originally Gothic, but was then remodelled in a baroque style. In 1780 it was once more transformed in neo-Gothic style.

Interior – White and bare, it has a nave and two aisles with a choir. Of note at the beginning of the right aisle is the *funerary monument of the archduchess Maria Christina* (Maria Theresa's favorite daughter who died in 1798), a neoclassic work

Augustinerkirche. Left, interior; right, the tomb
of Archduchess Maria Christina of Sachsen-Teschen,
by Antonio Canova.

Danublus-Brunnen: in the background
a view of the Albertina.

by Antonio Canova (1806) and the annexed **Chapel of St. George**, with two aisles. This church, like the others in the city, is a Hapsburg mausoleum. In a niche in the Chapel of St. George, closed by grills, is the **Herzgruft** (Heart Crypt) with 54 silver urns which contain the hearts of 54 members of the royal family. The «oldest» heart is that of Ferdinand II (1578-1637), the «youngest» is that of Archduke Francis Charles (1802-1878), father of the emperor Francis Joseph.

ALBERTINA – The palace, named after its founder, Duke Albrecht of Sachsen-Teschen, was built in 1801 and houses one of the largest collections of graphic art in the world, the **Graphische Sammlung**, with its 40,000 drawings and over a million prints. It contains works by Leonardo, Raphael, Rubens, Rembrandt, Cranach, Bruegel, Dürer and, among contemporaries, Picasso, Matisse, Chagall. Generally the most famous works can be seen, despite their fragility. Periodically, large exhibitions permit the public to see parts of the collection.

The flight of stairs that begins near the entrance to the museum leads to a terrace, dominated by the *equestrian monument to Duke Albrecht*, from which you can descend, on the other side, towards, the Burggarten once more (see page 36) for a well-earned and pleasant rest.

STAATSOPER

Haydn, Mozart, Beethoven, Schubert, Strauss: these names by themselves suffice to give an idea of the importance of Vienna in the history of music. Their works and those of many other composers still resound in this theater which, together with the Scala of Milan and the Metropolitan of New York, is considered the greatest lyric theater of the world, where sensational first-night performances, shows and great balls are held, making the spirit and style of imperial Vienna come alive more, perhaps, than anything else.

The construction of the grandiose building in Renaissance style, finished between 1861 and 1868, was the cause of bitter controversy which had tragic consequences for the two architects, E. van der Nüll and A. von Siccardsburg, the former committing suicide and the latter dying of a heart attack two months later. Neither one lived to see their project inaugurated, in 1869, with a performance of Mozart's «Don Giovanni».

In 1945 the theater was almost completely destroyed by aerial bombardments. Rebuilt and renewed, above all with the introduction of various modern technical devices in the stage, it can seat 2209 spectators.

Guided tours let the visitor admire the hall, the foyers and the stage. The large staircase decorated with *statues of the nine muses* by Joseph Gasser is quite imposing. The frescoes of the lunettes in the vestibule and the loggias, by Moritz von Schwind, are also lovely. They remained miraculously intact during the war. Outside twin fountains flank the palace.

**The 19th-century building in Renaissance
style of the Staatsoper.**

Behind the Opera another famous Viennese institution is to be found: **Hotel Sacher**, which has always been the rendezvous for the aristocracy of the empire and all the important people who happened to be passing through the city. This elegant establishment is also renowned for its restaurant and has lent its name to the famous Viennese cake, the «Sachertorte», as well as playing a part in secret meetings, political intrigues and love affairs which involved the aristocracy and political class of half of Europe.

KÄRNTNERSTRASSE

This broad street joins the Ring, at the level of the Opera, with St. Stephen's square. Closed to traffic and transformed into a delightful pedestrian zone several years ago, with the adjacent Graben it is the parlour of Vienna. Trees surrounded by benches are ideal places to rest; cafés and restaurants, which in summer flow over into the street with their tables, promote meetings and conversation; musicians, jugglers, clowns of all kinds provide entertainment, often of high level and for all tastes, to anyone who takes the time to amble along the street. Luxurious shops line the street where, if one likes, one can enjoy the special atmosphere of famous cafés, like «Sirk»'s, where «respectable» Viennese used to meet in the last years of the empire. A few meters from the beginning of the street, on the right, is the **Malteserkirche** (Church of the Knights of Malta), a small Gothic temple of the 14th century (with a neoclassic facade), in memory of the past of this medieval order of knights.

A short street to the left leads to the Neuer Markt (New Market) square. At the end, on the corner where Kärntnerstrasse meets the Graben, is the Stock im Eisen Platz with the curious **Stock im Eisen**, an old tree trunk covered with nails which it is said were hammered in by every blacksmith who passed that way.

A view of the elegant and lively Kärntnerstrasse.

Kaisergruft (Mausoleum of the Hapsburgs). Left,
the tomb of Francis Joseph; right, the tomb of
Maria Theresa and Francis of Lorraine.

KAISERGRUFT

A small baroque church, at one end of the **Neuer Markt** (New Market) and built in 1632, the **Kapuzinerkirche** (Capuchin Church) was where the Hapsburgs chose to hold the funeral rites for the members of the royal family.

Next to the church is a closed door. Ring the bell and you will be admitted to a long corridor and a narrow flight of stairs which leads to the Kaisergruft, the striking mausoleum of the Hapsburgs, where, since 1633, all the princes of royal blood have been buried, including 12 emperors and 15 empresses. In these ten bare and ghostly rooms the history of the Hapsburgs, of Austria, and in a sense of all of Europe, passes quickly by as one reads, one after the other, the names written over the bronze sepulchers which time and neglect are inexorably corroding and which must be continuously restored. Crowded one next to the other, often in bare sarcophaguses which are almost haphazardly piled up, 144 members of the Hapsburg family reign over their last empire, a solemn symbol of a grandiose past.

If we begin from the Gründergruft (Founders' crypt) to the right of the entrance, we find the tombs of Emperor Matthias and his wife Anna of Tyrol, those of Ferdinand III, of Leopold I, of Joseph I. From the old crypt there is an entrance to the Crypt of Maria Theresa, buried with her husband Francis I in a splendid baroque tomb, perhaps the loveliest in the entire mausoleum, by B.F. Moll. In the following four rooms among others repose the emperors Francis II, Leopold II, Ferdinand I and Maximilian of Mexico.

In the last crypt before the chapel and the exit, is the tomb of the last great emperor, Francis Joseph, who reigned for 68 years over Austria-Hungary, buried near his wife Elizabeth (Sissi) and his son Rudolf, both of whom died tragically.

Turning back, Donnergasse leads once more to the Kärntnerstrasse and from here towards the Himmelpfortgasse on the other side. At n. 8 is the **Winterpalais des Prinzen Eugen** (Winter Palace of Prince Eugene), a baroque masterpiece erected at the end of the 17th century by Fischer von Erlach the Elder, now occupied by the Ministry of Finance.
Almost opposite the palace, Rauhenstrasse and the evocative Ballgasse – a narrow lane flanked by fine perfectly restored buildings and prestigious places such as the «Ball» café at n. 5 – both lead towards the Franciscan Church.

FRANZISKANERKIRCHE

It was built between 1603 and 1611 by the Franciscan friars on the site of a precedent Franciscan convent. In Renaissance style, the church was remodelled in the 18th century.

Interior – With a nave only, it is decorated with works by important baroque artists: the monumental *high altar*, built in 1707, is by Andrea Pozzo, while the *organ*, set in the choir, was made by J. Wöckerl in 1642.
In the center of the charming **Franziskanerplatz** (Franciscan square) is the *Mosesbrunnen* (Moses Fountain) by J.M. Fischer, of 1798.

From the square, Grünaugergasse leads to Domgasse, which together with the nearby Blutgasse and the surrounding buildings is one of the best examples of redevelopment of the historical center. The old streets in disrepair to be found here only a few years ago have given way to a series of houses, courtyards and gardens, re-

Two old and famous houses in the city. On the left, the Figarohaus in the Domgasse; on the right, the Basiliskenhaus in the Schönlaterngasse.

developed, restored and amply supplied with shops, art galleries and cafés. At n. 5 Domgasse is the **Figarohaus**, where Mozart lived in 1784-1787, in the most fertile period of his artistic career. Here, among other things, he composed «The Marriage of Figaro», as commemorated in the memorial tablet on the back of the palace, overlooking Schulerstrasse. Today the house has been transformed into a small museum which contains various souvenirs of the great musician.

A few steps from Domgasse is Wollzeile, a long business street, full of shops and book stores. At n. 5 is a pretty passageway through the courtyards of the houses which leads to the cathedral square, and where one of the most famous restaurants in Vienna, the «Figlmüller» is to be found. Continuing along Wollzeile up to n. 35, where it crosses on the left with the Postgasse, is the **Dominikanerkirche** (Dominican Church), a fine baroque church of the 17th century, rebuilt by J. Spatz, C. Basino and A. Carnevale on the site of a precedent 13th- century building.

Not much further on, on the left, is the entrance to Schönlaterngasse.

Schönlaterngasse – The «street of the pretty lantern» which winds along lined by numerous and inviting cafés and beer halls, also contains some of the jewels of old Vienna. At n. 7 is the **Basiliskenhaus** (House of the Basilisk), one of the oldest bourgeois houses in the city, documented as far back as 1212, even if it was remodelled in the 16th and 18th centuries. The name of the building is tied to a legend concerning a small dragon generated by a rooster, whose terrible stratagems were defeated by the courage of a young baker who managed to transform it into stone. And this petrified image of the basilisk decorates the facade of the house. At n. 6 is the **Schöne Laterne** (Pretty Lantern), wrought in 1680, which gave the street its name.

HEILIGENKREUZERHOF

The entrance to this large courtyard, surrounded by splendid buildings of the 17th and 18th centuries, is at n. 5 Schönlaterngasse. For more than 700 years the courtyard has belonged to the monks of the famous monastery of Heiligenkreuz, not far

A view of Heiligenkreuzerhof.

Bernhardkapelle: interior.

from Vienna, near Mayerling castle. It was originally built as the city headquarters of the monks, and was later transformed into dwelling quarters. Little remains of the original medieval structure after the remodellings of 1660 and the 18th century which transformed the complex into what it is now. The peaceful atmosphere seems to invite one to pause and take a second look at each of the buildings which line this fabulous courtyard. To mention only one – the **Bernhardkapelle** (Chapel of St. Ber-

Jesuitenkirche: on the right the fresco by Andrea Pozzo with its trompe-l'oeil dome.

nard), a baroque masterpiece realized in 1660 and remodelled later. The *high altar* is by M. Altomonte, while the interior decorations are by Giovanni Giuliani.

Not far off three buildings of great importance from the historical-artistic point of view surround the simple lovely **Dr. Ignaz Seipelplatz**, center of the revolutionary movements of 1848 and now named after one of the first chancellors of the Austrian Republic in the twenties.

The **Jesuitenkirche** (Jesuit Church) dominates the square with a facade flanked by twin bell towers. Built in the midst of the Counter Reformation, between 1627 and 1631, the sumptuous interior is the work of Andrea Pozzo (early 18th century). The *high altar* and the *frescoes* of the vaulting with its trompe-l'oeil dome, are noteworthy.

To the left of the church is the **Akademie der Wissenschaften** (Academy of Sciences), a palace in baroque-rococo style built in 1753, commissioned from Jean-Nicolas Jadot de Ville-Issey by Francis I. The long facade is decorated with statues, and columns, and has a large balcony. There are fine fountains on either side of the main entrance. Inside one can visit the *fete hall*, frescoed by Gregorio Guglielmi. Unfortunately what we see is only a copy of the ceiling fresco. The original was destroyed in a fire in 1961. On the side opposite the Academy is the seat of the **Alte Universität** (Old University), built in the 17th century by the Jesuits (who at the time were in charge of teaching in the University) on the site of a 14th-century building.

From the square we can continue along **Backerstrasse**, a fine street with a wealth of palaces and interesting houses: among others at n. 7, one in Renaissance style of the 16th century, with a magnificent courtyard and loggias, well worth a visit; at n. 8 and at n. 16 are two examples of baroque buildings both built in the first half of the 18th century, under the influence of the works of the great architects of the time such as J.L. von Hildebrandt.

Across a small square named **Lugek** which is dominated by the monument to Gutenberg, one arrives at the oldest square in Vienna, the Hoher Markt.

**The Vermählungsbrunnen at the center
of the Hoher Markt square.**

The ingenious lever-clock on the Rotgasse arch.

HOHER MARKT

A large rectangular area surrounded by modern buildings – this is what the Old Market square now looks like. Most of it was destroyed in the fighting of April 1945. But notwithstanding the war, something of the old square, which was the center of the city for centuries, has come down to our times. First of all at n. 3, on the left side of the square, can be seen the remains of two Roman houses discovered after the war. They were probably part of the antique forum of Vindobona, on the site of the praetor's palace, the most important building in the Roman citadel. This may be the very spot where Marcus Aurelius, the philosopher-emperor, a lucid and impassioned eye-witness of his time, sojourned and died in 180 A.D.

The baroque **Vermählungsbrunnen** (Fountain of the Wedding of the Virgin), built on a project by J.E. Fischer von Erlach the Younger in 1732, conspicuously marks the center of the square. The fountain, which Charles VI had made to replace one that had fallen into ruin, consists of a small temple in white marble with a group representing the marriage of Mary and Joseph.

In the right corner of the square, there is, lastly, one of the loveliest and oddest products of Viennese Art Nouveau. In 1913 F. von Matsch designed and executed a mechanical clock, the **Ankeruhr** (lever-clock) for the arch of the Rotgasse where each hour is marked by the passage of figures from Austrian history. If you happen to be in the square at noon, be sure to stop and watch the complete parade of figures.

Two views of the splendid baroque facades of the Altes Rathaus
(left) and the Böhmische Hofkanzlei (right).

ALTES RATHAUS

From the square, Wipplingerstrasse leads to this old building at
n. 8, which was the seat of the city government from 1316 on.
It was often renewed in the following centuries, and housed the
municipal offices until 1885, when they were transferred to the
new palace on the Ring. Its baroque facade dates to 1699 and
betrays the influence of J.B. Fischer von Erlach. In the central
court is the lovely **Andromedabrunnen** (Andromeda Fountain)
of 1741, the last work of G.R. Donner: a wrought iron balcony
overhangs a lead relief of Andromeda with Perseus killing the
dragon.

On the other side of the street, at n. 7, is the palace of the **Böhmische Hofkanzlei**,
the ex Court Chancellery of Bohemia, a baroque work by J.B. Fischer von Erlach,
realized between 1709 and 1714. In 1751 it was enlarged by M. Gerl. The caryat-
ids on the portals and the fine statues on the facade, by Lorenzo Mattielli, are of
interest.
The back of the palace faces on **Judenplatz**, center of the old Hebrew ghetto in
the Middle Ages.

MARIA AM GESTADE

Continuing along Wipplingerstrasse, a side street on the left
leads to the small old Church of S. Mary on the Banks.
As indicated by the name, the church once stood along an arm
of the Danube, which disappeared centuries ago. Earliest mention of the church is in documents of 1158. Destroyed in a fire

of 1258, it was immediately rebuilt, but was then once more destroyed. After various vicissitudes it finally took on its present aspect between 1397 and 1414. Damaged again in the two Turkish sieges and then neglected for centuries, it was restored once for all in the 18th century on the orders of Emperor Francis I.

In Gothic style, the exterior seems to be squeezed between the surrounding houses and reaching skywards, almost as if that were the only free space left. The bell tower is a masterpiece of Gothic art by M. Knab: polygonal in plan, with seven sides, and 56 meters high, it is topped by a splendid openwork spire which makes the whole tower seem light and delicate.

Inside, a nave flanked by pilasters and a deep choir, and numerous fine works of art: part of a triptych of 1460 is visible in a small chapel on the right. It is by the Master of Maria Stiegen and represents the *Coronation of the Virgin* and the *Annunciation*. At the entrance to the choir are 14th-century *statues*. The high altar, a neo-Gothic work of 1846 is more recent. And last but not least the splendid *stained-glass windows* in the choir which date to the 14th century.

A brief walk along the street flanking the church, Salvatorgasse, on which the back of the Altes Rathaus faces, and then along Marc Aurelstrasse, leads us to one of the oldest zones of the city.

The picturesque church of Maria am Gestade.

A narrow flight of steps and a lane, the Sterngasse, lead to the **Fleischmarkt**. The ancient meat market and point of encounter for the Greek traders who arrived in the city is today a fine long street lined with taverns, beer halls and art galleries. Among them is the famous «Griechenbeisel» (Greek tavern) at n. 11 in an old house of medieval origin which already existed in the 15th century and was the favorite meeting place for many famous personages.

RUPRECHTSKIRCHE

Halfway up the Fleischmarkt the short Rabenstrasse and then the Seitenstettengasse (where the 19th-century Synagogue of Vienna is located) lead us towards the splendid terraced little square in front of the small Church of St. Rupert.

This is the oldest church in Vienna. According to legend, it was built in 740 by two disciples of St. Rupert. Actually the oldest parts of the building, the nave and the lower part of the bell tower, date to the 11th century, while the additions are of the 15th century.

The exterior, bare and simple, is covered with ivy. It is dominated by the Romanesque bell tower with two-light windows. **Inside** there are various fine works in the Gothic aisles: the organ balustrade, of 1439, the fine 13th-century *stained-glass window* in the choir, with a Crucifixion, and the paintings of the high altar, representing *St. Rupert*, by J.M. Rottmayr (1708).

The evocative little square which surrounds the church faces on Franz Josefs-Kai, the avenue which goes along the Donaukanal and can be reached via a flight of stairs.

The oldest church in Vienna: Ruprechtskirche.

RING

A ring of tree-lined boulevards four kilometers long and 60 meters wide, together with the Donaukanal, encloses the historic and monumental center of Vienna, changing its name from one place to the next as it goes along (Stubenring, Parkring, Schubertring, Kärntnerring, Opernring, Burgring, Dr. Karl Renner-Ring, Dr. Karl Lueger-Ring, Schottenring).

It was Emperor Francis Joseph in 1857 who ordered the demolition of the old city walls which still enclosed the city center so that the city could be provided with a street that was worthy of the capital of a great empire.

The Ring – or Ringstrasse as the Viennese call the circumvallation that was created along the line of the old fortifications – immediately became the main street of the city, where the upper classes and the Austrian aristocracy chose to build their palaces, near the large public buildings which began to rise up along the boulevards. The result was an impressive parade of palaces and symbols of power, most of which were colored «Schönbrunn or emperor yellow», set in the midst of uniquely beautiful parks and gardens and alternated with squares and monuments. Differing in style, these buildings all manifested the pomp and grandeur of an empire which was heading towards an irreversible crisis and a rapid dispersal just as its most important symbols were being raised along the Ring. The irony of history has no limits.

Even today to walk or slowly drive along the Ring in a horse cab is a pleasant suggestive experience, which inevitably recalls to mind imperial splendours of times gone by. A long row of palaces, characterized by a monumental style which imitates the great buildings of the past (classical, Gothic, Renaissance) line the avenues: from the Opera to the palaces which house the Kunsthistorisches and the Naturhistorisches Museum, to the Burgtheater, Parliament, the City Hall, the University, the Votivkirche. And including various splendid parks such as the Stadtpark, the Burggarten, the Vorksgarten and the Rathauspark.

The loveliest part of the city-line road begins at the Opera. On Burgring the **Burgtor** (or External Gate) indicates the entrance to Heldenplatz and the imperial palace. Built in 1824 to replace the ancient fortifications destroyed during the Napoleonic occupation of 1809, it was transformed into a monument to the heroes and the war dead in 1934.

MARIA THERESIENPLATZ

Opposite the royal palace, at the level of the Burgtor, the Ring broadens out into one of the most majestic scenographies of the entire city. Separated by flower beds and basins decorated with statues, the two buildings which house the Museums of Art and of Natural Science stand like imposing mirror images, both

topped by tall domes and with Renaissance facades decorated
with statues and columns.

Built between 1872 and 1891 by Gottfried Semper and Karl von
Hasenauer, they were destined from the very beginning for the
imperial collections.

Inside, the rooms are decorated with frescoes by the most important artists of the time, such as G. Klimt, Makart and Munkaczy.

In the center of the square is the large **monument to Maria Theresa**, finished after 13 years of work, in 1887. A large group includes the empress at whose feet are gathered the most famous
figures of her time – her husband, her faithful counselor Kaunitz,
her generals and famous men such as Mozart and Haydn who
made her reign so great. The square is shut off by the **Messepalast** (Fair Building) which formerly housed the imperial stables
and was designed by Fischer von Erlach, father and son (between 1723 and 1725). The building, with its long facade of
about 320 meters and with various pavilions, is at present used
for trade fairs, exhibitions, fashion shows. Inside, half hidden, is
one of the most famous and pleasant restaurants («Beisel») in
Vienna, the «Glacisbeisel».

KUNSTHISTORISCHES MUSEUM

Like any self-respecting reigning house, the Hapsburgs collected works of art of all kinds. Throughout the centuries thousands of objects and paintings were continuously added to the royal collections, constituting the base of what is one of the greatest art museums in the world.

The visitor who intends to follow in the tracks of imperial Vienna cannot help but pay a visit to this museum which contains thousands of true masterpieces.

Organized in 91 rooms, disposed on three floors, it unites four outstanding collections: the collection of Egyptian and antique art, the collection of sculpture and applied arts, the picture gallery, the numismatic collection.

MEZZANINE – to the right of the entrance hall begin the rooms of the **Collection of Egyptian and Antique Art**, with almost 4000 items on exhibit. **Room I**: large sarcophagus in black granite of the Ptolemaic period. **Room II**: funerary stelae and mummies of animals. **Rooms III-IV-V**: sculpture, funerary statuettes, bronzes, mummies. **Room VI**: mastaba or *funerary chamber of Prince Kaninisut*, from Giza (2800-2400 ca. B.C.) **Rooms VII-VIII**: collection of vases from the Cretan-Mycenaean period (1400 B.C.) and from Magna Graecia. **Room IX**: Tanagra figurines (4th-3rd cent. B.C.), Cypriote terra-cottas. **Room X**: *Amazon sarcophagus* (Greece, 4th cent. B.C.). **Room XI-XII**: Greco-Roman sculpture, Greek bronzes, mosaics of the 2nd cent. A.D. **Rooms XIII-XIV**: Greek sculpture of the 5th and 4th centuries; noteworthy the terra-cotta statue of *Athena*, from Rocca d'Aspromonte (5th cent. B.C.). Bronzes, Etruscan vases. **Room XV**: collection of Roman art. Series of cameos of the 1st-3rd cent. A.D., including the famous *Gemma Augustea* (1st cent.), representing the apotheosis of the Emperor Augustus. **Rooms XVI-XVII**: Byzantine and early medieval objects, Germanic gold objects from the 5th

Kunsthistorisches Museum: facade.

David Teniers the Younger: «Archduke Leopold William
in his Gallery in Brussels» (1655).

century. **Room XVIII**: *treasure of Nagy-Szent-Miklos*, or Attila's treasure, composed of 23 pieces in gold from Hungary (proto-Bulgarian art of the 9th cent.). The left wing contains the rich **Collection of Sculpture and Applied Arts**. These include, among others, a splendid series of *Flemish and French tapestries*, altogether almost 900 pieces, of which about 50 are exhibited in rotation. In addition to the Brussels manufacture, which is by far the most important, are works from Arras, Tournai, Bruges, Enghien, Antwerp, Delft, Leyden, Haarlem. **Rooms XIX-XX**: works of the Austrian baroque and the rococo. Furniture, glassware and equestrian statuettes in ivory, portraying Austrian emperors, made by M. Steinl between 1662 and 1664. **Room XXII**: examples of German, Dutch, Italian baroque. **Rooms XXIV-XXV**: bowls and vases in semi-precious stone and precious metals, 16th and 17th centuries; examples of German goldsmith work. **Room XXVI**: *Michael beaker*, French, 1530, in gold and precious stones. **Room XXVII**: *bronzes* by Giambologna and the *salt cellar* in gold by Benvenuto Cellini, made in 1540 at the request of Francis I. **Room XXVIII**: bronzes and examples of German gold work of the 15th-16th centuries. **Rooms XXIX-XXX-XXXI**: glass, bronzes and sculpture of the Italian school, 15th-16th centuries. **Room XXXII**: putto of a Florentine school (15th cent.); school of Della Robbia, Desiderio da Settignano (*Laughing Boy*) and Francesco Laurana (*bust of Isabella of Aragon*, late 15th century). **Rooms XXXIII-XXXVI**: Gothic ivories and sculpture from the 14th and 15th centuries, including the *Falconer* by A. Pilgram, the *Krumauer Madonna* (wooden sculpture by G. Erhart), *Allegory of Vanity* (ca. 1500); Byzantine 9th-century ivories; goldsmith work. **Room XXXVII**: German clocks of the 16th century.
Theseus and the Minotaur by Antonio Canova are on the flight of stairs that leads to the upper floors.

FIRST FLOOR – The 15 rooms (Roman numerals) and the 24 cabinets (Arabic numerals) are completely taken up by the Picture Gallery. Around 1600 works by German, Flemish, Dutch, Italian, Spanish and French masters comprise the imposing

54

Canaletto: «Vienna from the Belvedere» (1759-60). Below:
head of the pharaoh Sesostris III (Middle Kingdom,
XII dynasty, ca. 1850 B. C.).

55

Benvenuto Cellini: Salt Cellar (1540-43).

collection. **Room I**: works by Titian (*Ecce Homo*, 1545; *Portrait of Pope Paul III Farnese*). **Cabinet 1**: Mantegna (*St. Sebastian*) and Giorgione (*Adoration of the Shepherds; The Three Philosophers*). **Room II**: paintings by Tintoretto (*Susanna and the Elders; St. Jerome*). **Cabinet 2**: works by Titian and Lorenzo Lotto. **Room III**: Paolo Veronese (*Judith*). **Cabinet 3**: Tintoretto (*Christ at the Column*). **Cabinets 4-5-6**: works by Jacopo Bassano, Perugino, Raphael (*Madonna del Prato*, 1505). **Cabinet 7**: Andrea del Sarto (*Pietà*). **Room IV**: works by Italian baroque painters, including Guido Reni. **Cabinet 8**: canvases by Parmigianino and Correggio. **Room V**: Italian 17th-century painters such as Caracciolo and Caravaggio (*Madonna of the Rosary; David with the Head of Goliath*). **Cabinets 8-10-11**: canvases by Poussin, Schönfeld and Feti. Numerous portraits of the Hapsburgs. **Room VI**: Luca Giordano, Giambattista Tiepolo (*Death of Brutus*). **Cabinet 12**: portraits by Velázquez (*The Infanta Margherita Teresa; Don Filippo Próspero*). **Room VII**: large canvases by Bernardo Bellotto representing 18th-century Vienna; David (*Napoleon Crossing the Alps*). **Cabinet 13**: works by F. Guardi, Tiepolo, Canaletto. **Room VIII**: Flemish painters (J. Van Eyck; R. van Der Weyden; H. Memling). **Cabinet 14**: Bosch (*Ascent to Calvary*). **Room IX**: Dutch 17th-century painters. **Cabinet 15**: works by A. Dürer (*Adoration of the Trinity; Portrait of Maximilian I*). **Room X**: perhaps the largest collection of works by Peter Bruegel the Elder, one of the masters of Flemish art (*Peasant Wedding, Slaughter of the Innocents, Tower of Babel; Carnival and Lent; Hunters in the Snow; Children's Games; Calvary*). **Room XI**: Van Dyck (*Fish Market*); Jordaens. **Cabinet 16**: Cranach the Elder (*Crucifixion; St. Jerome*). **Cabinet 17**: Cranach the Younger and Cranach the Elder, Albrecht Altdorfer. **Cabinet**

18: portraits by Hans Holbein the Younger. **Cabinet 19**: Arcimboldo, Spranger. **Room XII**: various portraits by Anton van Dyck. **Cabinet 20**: canvases by Rubens (*Self-Portrait; Girl with a Fur*, 1638). **Rooms XIII-XIV**: works by Peter Paul Rubens (*Portrait of Helena Fourment; Ildefonsus altarpiece*). **Cabinets 21-22**: works by Teniers the Younger, portraits by Franz Hals. **Cabinet 23**: Rembrandt (*His Mother; Self-Portrait*). **Room XV**: Dutch landscape painters (Ruisdael); Rembrandt (*Apostle Paul*). **Cabinet 24**: Jan Vermeer van Delft (*Allegory of Painting*).

SECOND FLOOR – A fine series of *tapestries* can be seen here. The **Münzenkabinett** is housed in some of the rooms. It is a numismatic collection of great worth, including coins and medals of all periods, with about 2000 pieces on exhibit.

NATURHISTORISCHES MUSEUM

Francis Stephen I, Maria Theresa's husband and passionately interested in science, as well as being a collector, began the collection of minerals and objects pertaining to the natural sciences on which the museum's collection is still based. In 1889 Emperor Francis Joseph officially inaugurated the prestigious collection, which continued to be enriched with purchases, research campaigns and acquisitions from various sources.

Today, with about 11 million items, the Naturhistorisches Museum can be numbered among the largest of its kind in the world.

Divided into eight sectors (mineralogy, geology, palaeontology, vertebrates, invertebrates, botany, anthropology, prehistory) the museum covers two floors.

MEZZANINE – An unbelievable collection of marvels awaits the visitor who approaches the 19th-century show cases or wanders through the richly frescoed rooms. Precious minerals, gigantic stones, meteorites, prehistoric fossils, human skulls 35,000 years old form a kaleidoscope of images, continuously provoking exclamations of wonder and surprise.

Rooms 1-5: systematic collection of minerals from all parts of the world, of meteorites and precious stones, including an *opal* which weighs 117 kilos, the largest *platinum nugget* ever found (a little over 5 kilos), a *salt obelisk* which weighs 1680 kilos, fragments of alexandrite which change color when exposed to fluorescent light, a *fragment of the moon* brought to earth by Apollo 17 in 1972, and all sorts of diamonds, gold and silver nuggets, crystals from Japan. In the room of precious stones (n. 4) there is an incredible *bouquet of jewels and precious stones* of all kinds (about 2700 all in all), given by Maria Theresa to her husband Francis in 1760, and some Colombian emeralds of absolute purity. In room 5 there is a collection of meteorites. **Rooms 6-10**: here prehistoric flora and fauna illustrate the evolution of life on our planet in the Palaeozoic, Mesozoic and Tertiary periods. In room 6 are exhibited the oldest fossil plants. Room 10 is particularly fine and impressive with its life-size reproductions of the great dinosaurs of the Mesozoic period (from 250 to 65 million years ago).

The **corridors near the staircase** house a rich display of the Glacial Era (Pleistocene: from 1,8 million to 12,000 years ago), explaining causes and evolution. Examples of European and American fauna are to be seen.

Rooms 11-15: collection of finds and hand-made objects from the Stone Age on, such as the famous *Willendorf Venus*, a limestone statuette made 20-30,000 years ago, and the collection of objects from the Hallstatt culture (800-500 B.C.), including a beautiful richly decorated funerary cart (room 14).

Rooms 16-17: in the anthropological section hundreds of human skulls reconstruct the exact evolution of the species in the «last» 35,000 years and testify to the differences between the various extant races.

Room 18: reserved for children: with illustrative panels, reproductions of animals and typical Austrian dwellings which introduce children to the great themes of natural history, in terms of play and entertainment.

FIRST FLOOR – In the botany and zoology section an enormous number of items and stuffed animals are preserved. They include practically all living species and many that have long been extinct.

Room 21: this is the famous *Viennese herbarium*, where more than 2 million plants are collected. Illustrative plates explain the various aspects of plant life.

Rooms 22-24: dedicated to the invertebrates. Tens of thousands of molluscs, spiders, crustaceans, insects.

Rooms 25-39: dedicated to the vertebrates. Fish, birds, reptiles, mammals, comprise this enormous and fantastic immobile zoo. Since some of these species have been extinct for some time, the examples exhibited represent invaluable evidence of the animal world (noteworthy are the dodo, the Tasmanian tiger and the giant panda).

PARLIAMENT

One need not know much about art to recognize the cultural-artistic inspiration for this building by Theophil von Hansen: ancient Greece and its temples are reborn in an imposing edifice with a pronaos and a pediment, and while there may be some question as to its beauty, as is the case with all imitations, it is undoubtedly spectacular. Finished in 1883, the palace was, until 1918, the seat of the Council of State. When the republic was proclaimed it came to house the two legislative chambers of Austria, the National Council and the Federal Council. The columned porch of the main facade is preceded by a staircase consisting of two flights of stairs decorated with horse tamers in bronze and numerous Greek and Roman personages. Below the staircase, right at the center of the square, is the large monumental **Fountain of Pallas Athena** more than four meters tall with the goddess of wisdom holding a statue of Nike, the goddess of victory, in her hand and surrounded by other allegorical figures.

The neoclassic facade of Parliament.

The Burgtheater: one of the most prestigious
theaters in the world.

BURGTHEATER

In 1776 Emperor Joseph II founded the «National and Court
Theater» which at the time had its headquarters on the Michaelerplatz. In 1888 the present building, designed by Gottfried
Semper, was built and it quickly became one of the most important theater buildings in German-speaking countries.
Like so many important buildings in Vienna the theater was seri-
ously damaged in the last war. Restored and modernized, it has
preserved at least part of its old charm. Of interest are *paintings*
by G. Klimt and F. Matsch on the side staircases, which survived
the bombings. The Burgtheater is only one, even if it is the most
prestigious, of the many prose theaters in Vienna (about 15 are
permanently active during the theater season which generally
goes from September through June). The Akademietheater, the
Theater in der Josefstadt, the Volkstheater are some of the most
distinguished names which offer a rich variety of classic and
modern plays.

RATHAUS

An iron warrior may very well be the most authentic symbol of
Vienna. With his sword and banner he watches over the fate of
the city and its government from the top of the central tower of
the town hall, 104 meters high.
The offices of the mayor and the City Council are in one of the
most important civic buildings in neo-Gothic style in Vienna. Between 1872 and 1883 Friedrich von Schmidt provided the city
with this austere and imposing municipal palace. The facade is

characterized by four spires 61 meters high and the pinnacled tower on which the *Rathausmann* keeps watch. Two and a half meters high and made of almost four tons of metal, he was built in 1882 by the master smith Alexander Nehr as a symbol of Vienna as well as serving as a lightning rod.

Various rooms **inside** are open to the public and worth a visit, including the Schmidt Room, the room for the meetings of the City Council, with its imposing bronze chandelier ten meters high and with 254 lights, and the large Fest hall.

In one of the seven internal courtyards, the **Arkadenhof**, open-air concerts are held every summer as part of the Viennese music summer.

Rathauspark: in the background the slender silhouette of the central tower of the Town Hall.

A small but magnificent park, the **Rathauspark**, runs along in front of the town hall, connecting it to the Ring. It is only one of the multitude of shady well-kept gardens which are an integral part of this city: exotic trees, each one labeled with its name; fountains surrounded by neat rows of chairs to be used by visitors; statues and monuments (including those to the waltz kings, Johann Strauss father and Joseph Lanner, and those to the eight great figures of Austrian history in the central boulevard); trim inviting lanes, are the typical ingredients of these delightful green oases.

UNIVERSITÄT

A few steps further on, the massive neo-Renaissance building of the University, built by Heinrich von Ferstel between 1873 and 1884, is to be encountered on Dr. Karl Lueger- Ring.

It is one of the oldest universities in central Europe, for it was founded in 1365 by Duke Rudolf IV to augment the development and importance of the city. Under the enlightened reign of Maria Theresa it was reorganized and potentiated. At present it is a modern University with thousands of students who make use of its monumental halls (such as the great fete hall, with the statues of the two deserving sovereigns) and its spacious courtyards. The central court is particularly pleasant: an extensive portico decorated with busts of docents encloses 3000 square meters of flower beds and shady meadows, with a fountain at the center, the **Kastaliabrunnen**, by E. Hellmer (1910).

Left: the monumental Renaissance building of the old university.
Right: the new headquarters.

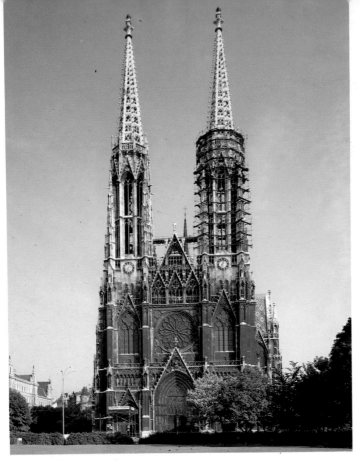

Votivkirche.

VOTIVKIRCHE

Like all self-respecting emperors the Hapsburgs were the object of many attempts at assassination, some of which «hit the mark», In one of these, in 1853, the then young Emperor Francis Joseph I fortunately eluded his assassin's dagger, and his brother, the future and less fortunate emperor of Mexico Maximilian I, had this church built on the site of the attempt as thanks for the averted danger.

The Votivkirche is the first example of a post-baroque religious building in Vienna. The architect Heinrich von Ferstel built the church using the 13th-century French Gothic cathedrals as his inspiration. Two towers 99 meters high frame the facade with its richly ornate portal. **Inside** the *16th-century mausoleum of Count Niklas Salm*, defender of Vienna during the Turkish siege of 1529 (in the last chapel on the left), and a wooden sculpture of Flemish school (probably from Antwerp, 15th century), with *scenes of the Passion* (in the chapel to the right of the high altar), are worthy of note.

MINORITENPLATZ

Turning back towards the imperial palace, behind the Burgtheater, we encounter Minoritenplatz. Considered one of the most aristocratic squares in Vienna, it is today one of the centers of Austrian political life. Three important buildings face on the square: at n. 3 is **Palais Dietrichstein**, built in the 17th century and remodelled in 1755 by L.F. Hillebrandt, at present seat of the Austrian Foreign Ministry; at n. 4 is the fine side portal by Gabriele de Gabrieli of **Palais Liechtenstein** (winter residence of the princely family), whose main entrance is on Burggasse. It was built between 1694 and 1706 on designs by D. Martinelli and still today belongs to the princes of Liechtenstein. At n. 5 is the 17th-century **Palais Starhemberg** where, in 1701, Count Starhemberg, who defended Vienna during the second Turkish siege of 1683, died. Today it is the seat of the Ministry of Public Education and Sciences.

Minoritenkirche: G. Raffaelli, copy of Leonardo's «Last Supper» (1804).

MINORITENKIRCHE

Built between 1339 and the end of the 14th century, damaged during the Turkish sieges and retouched and remodelled various times in the baroque period, it was finally restored in its original Gothic forms by Ferdinand von Hohenberg in 1789. Isolated at the center of the square, with a very steep roof, the imposing facade has a striking **main doorway** by the Parisian Friar Jakobus. The interior is divided into three aisles by eight columns. Of interest, in the left aisle, is a copy in mosaic of Leonardo's *Last Supper*, made by G. Raffaelli in 1804.

Entering the Herrengasse from the Minoritenplatz, in the 18th century Mollard-Clary Palace, one finds the **Niederösterreichisches Landesmuseum** (Museum of Lower Austria) with its two floors documenting in detail, the origins and culture of this part of the country. Meriting particular attention are the sections dedicated to artifacts from the Roman as well as preceding ages and to the exhibition of typical rural crafts (furniture, clothing and ceramics). The second-floor history and culture sections house paintings by Kokoschka, Schele and by the baroque artists Rottmayr, Martino Altomonte and Kremser Schmidt.

SCHÖNBRUNN CASTLE

Imagine if you can a long row of horse carriages taking the royal family of Vienna to their summer residence. Then have fun imagining the comings and goings of the members of the court in the sumptuous ball rooms, the servants at work, the empress and her ladies-in-waiting taking walks in the park. And if you can't quite imagine it all, help yourself with period prints or with the lovely pictures painted by Canaletto around the middle of the 18th century: this was Schönbrunn, the Versailles of the Hapsburgs, perhaps not the loveliest, but surely the most famous of the royal Austrian palaces.

Today, much more simply, it takes only a few minutes to get there on line 4 of the subway, which connects what is at this point nothing more than a city park with the historical center. From the small station (look at it carefully: in perfect Art Nouveau, it is by the great architect Otto Wagner), an avenue leads to the entrance of the palace, marked by two obelisks surmounted by the imperial eagle.

HISTORY

In the middle of the 16th century Emperor Maximilian II acquired a castle surrounded by a vast tract of land, the Katterburg. For over a century the property was almost forgotten by the Hapsburgs and not until 1672 was it decided to turn the Katterburg into a fine summer residence. Unfortunately fate had other things in store: in fact only a few years later, in 1683, the Turks who were besieging Vienna destroyed the castle and the park.

After the war, Emperor Leopold I was finally able to turn to more pacific undertakings which could also represent the power and ambitions of an empire that had de-

Schönbrunn Castle from the park.

M. Van Meytens: portrait of Empress
Maria Theresa at 60 years of age.

feated the Ottoman Turks. He commissioned the architect Fischer von Erlach to plan a large palace for the devastated park right outside Vienna. The architect outdid himself: the hill now occupied by the Gloriette was to be the site of a castle that was grander and larger than Versailles itself – Versailles, the coveted symbol of the powerful French monarchy. But the war had emptied the State treasury and von Erlach himself was forced to prepare an alternative design, elaborating the essential lines of the present castle.

Even though it was now smaller, the building of the castle continued slowly for various decades, until Maria Theresa, in 1743, commissioned Nikolaus Pacassi to finish the construction, adapting the original plans to the tastes of the time.

Maria Theresa and her 16 children used Schönbrunn as their habitual residence, and their personality is reflected in the castle and the park. Her son, Joseph II, who paid less attention to pomp and luxury than his mother, concentrated his interests on the park, addressing himself to the scientific aspect with the creation of the zoo and the botanical gardens.

In the centuries that followed Schönbrunn remained practically the same and was the scene of glorious and dramatic episodes of Austrian history. In 1805 and 1809 Napoleon set up his general headquarters here and it was in these rooms that the Austrian surrender was signed in 1809. When Napoleon fell, his son from his marriage to Maria Luisa, Napoleon Franz Joseph, the «king of Rome», lived here practically as a prisoner until he died of tuberculosis in 1832. In 1848, at the time of Francis Joseph, the castle once more began to be used as the habitual residence until the death of the emperor in 1916. The century-long Hapsburg monarchy came to an end in these rooms on November 11, 1918. Charles I signed his abdication papers, thus preparing the way for the Republic. Recently the castle of Schönbrunn has been the stage for great international happenings such as the meeting between John Kennedy and Nikita Khrushchev, on June 3, 1961.

THE CASTLE

A visitor arriving from the Schönbrunner Schloss-Strasse sees the castle as a long rather low building, painted in a tone of yellow which is known as «Schönbrunn or emperor yellow».

A fine rococo wrought iron gate, flanked by two obelisks, leads

Schönbrunn: Hall of Mirrors.

into the large **Court of honor**, a spacious area surrounded on three sides by buildings in typical 17th-century style used for parades and open-air fetes. In the right wing is the small but sumptuos **castle theater**, by N. Pacassi (1747) which still today is used for performances every summer. At the center of the sober facade the main entrance is surmounted by columns and leads to the imperial apartments and the park.

STATE APARTMENTS – Only 45 of the more than 1400 rooms of the castle are open to the public (guided visits in various languages), but they are enough to provide an illuminating cross section of the life style of the Hapsburgs and the taste of the period, of Maria Theresa's love for exotic elegant rooms, the restrained simplicity of Francis Joseph, and the luxury of the rooms of state.

The white and gold decorations, in rococo style, which characterize the apartments are the work of N. Pacassi. Of note also the large tile stoves, which were stoked from service corridors so that the servants could keep the fires going without bothering princes and courtiers.

The visit begins in the 10 rooms of **Francis Joseph's apartments**. He was known for his Spartan life and his reluctance to accept anything new and it is said that he was contrary to the arrival of electricity in the castle. His personality is reflected in the simplicity of the furnishings. The emperor died in his military field bed on November 21, 1916.

The state apartments and the private **Apartments of Maria Theresa** are completely different, and luxury, splendor and a taste for details fuse and create interiors of unrivalled sumptuousness, visible expressions of a woman who was as great and powerful as her empire. Tapestries, porcelains, chandeliers, paintings, chinoiserie, elaborate furniture in precious materials fill these rooms, among which particular attention should be paid to the **Hall of Mirrors**, where the child Mozart gave a concert for Maria Theresa; the **Vieux Laque Room**, with its walls lined with painted lacquer panels; the **Chinese Cabinets**, decorated with Chinese *porcelain* of the Ming period and ideal places for secret rendezvous and political conversations; the small fascinating **Porcelain Cabinet**, so-called because of wood carving, very like porcelain; the **Millions Room**, which is what the decorations cost, panelled in rare Chinese rosewood and set with *Persian and Indian miniatures* of the 16th century; the **Grand Gallery**, 43 luxurious meters reserved for the great fetes and important meetings.

On the ground floor of the palace, to the left of the main entrance, are other rooms which however can be seen only on special occasions. These are the so-called **Bergl Rooms**, where Maria Theresa loved to pass the time on hot summer days, frescoed with floral themes, tropical plants and animals by Johann Bergl, between 1769 and 1777.

Two precious rooms in the castle: left, the Vieux Laque Room; right, a Chinese cabinet.

Schönbrunn: the Blue Room.

THE PARK – The visitor is fascinated even more by the park than by the palace. Almost as large as the central district of Vienna, this garden with its 120 hectares, created in imitation of the French parks and often remodelled, is an ideal place for a long walk, perhaps after one has spent the morning seeing palaces and museums.

Aimlessly wandering, finally free of guides and escorts, it is easy to surrender to the romantic atmosphere of the long shady paths that unexpectedly bring you to a fountain or an unlikely Roman ruin. Dozens of squirrels come to beg a peanut or, unmindful of the passerby, chase each other through the trees and meadows

The delicate silhouette of the Gloriette reflected
in the still waters of the pool.

One of the foutains of the Naiad sculpted by Wilhelm Beyer.

which are interspersed with ponds, statues, baroque pavilions.

Upon leaving the castle the eye is almost inevitably drawn to the great neoclassic portico which dominates the hill in front of the palace. The **Gloriette** – as it is called – was built, as was much of the decoration of the park, by Ferdinand von Hohenberg in 1780, in memory of Kolin's victory of 1757. Weighed down with decorations that include trophies, heads of animals, suits of armor, 95 meters long and 19 meters high, it is the best spot from which to get a splendid panorama of the park and the castle against a background of the historical center of Vienna.

The romantic Fountain of the Roman Ruins
with the statues of the river god Elbe and the river
goddess Moldau in the foreground.

Two examples of the elegant architecture
in the park of Schönbrunn: left, the splendid Palmenhaus;
right, the refined central Pavilion.

Let us therefore wind our way towards this softly rolling hill
through the neat flower beds, where the flowers are renewed
three times a year (in spring only tulips are planted: thousands of
bulbs are sent expressly from Holland – a sign of the ancient and
profound ties between the north-European country and Vienna
and Austria). At the foot of the slope is the great **Neptune
Fountain** (1780) which suitably closes the parterre in front of the
castle.
A path quickly leads us to the Gloriette and from here, going right
(looking at the palace) we descend in the midst of the woods to
a make-believe Roman ruin and the delightful pavilion of the
Schöner Brunnen (from which the castle takes its name), or
Lovely Fountain. To the left, an avenue that once more crosses
the central parterre, leads to the entrance of the **Zoo**, which Francis Stephen of Lorraine, Maria Theresa's husband, had built in
1752 as the court menagerie. It was later enlarged by his son,
Emperor Joseph II, and is perhaps the only example in the world
of a baroque zoo. The original layout, while preserved and restored, has recently been renewed on modern criteria so that it
is better suited to housing the thousands of animals which crowd
the enclosures. Not far from the zoo is another of the jewels of
the park, the **Botanischer Garten** (Botanic Garden) with the **Palmenhaus**, the largest greenhouse for palms in Europe, built in
1880 by the architect F. von Segenschmid in glass and metal.
Nearby, in the midst of flowerbeds and meadows, a solar clock
and statues of Francis I and of Joseph II complete this enchanting
corner which is often crowded with children and old ladies looking for a bit of sun and peace.

The imperial coach entirely decorated in gold
in keeping with Rococo taste.

WAGENBURG – The Museum of Royal Coaches, one of the largest collections of its kind in the world, occupies the old coach-house in the right wing of the palace (entering from the Court of Honor). Sedan-chairs and harnesses, sleighs and gigs from the 17th to the 19th centuries include historical pieces such as the 18th-century **imperial coach** used for coronations, the **funerary coach of the Empress Elizabeth** or the gig especially built for Napoleon's son.

At the beginning of Mariahilfer Strasse, a few hundred yards from the Schönbrunn castle, is the **Technische Museum** with a complete panorama of the evolution of technology, industry and the contributions of Austrian scientists on its three floors. Among the items exhibited here are: the first sewing machine (Madersperger, 1830), the oldest typewriter (Mitterhofer, 1860), the steam machine by Cugnot (1770) and one of the first original models by the Wright brothers (1903).

A room in the Coach Museum (Wagenburg).

THE CASTLE OF BELVEDERE

HISTORY

In 1683 the Turks laid siege to Vienna for the second time. As had been the case a century and a half before, the city's defense against the Ottoman assault became the symbol of Christian resistence against Islamic expansionism.

From his residence in Brussels Prince Eugene of Savoy rushed to the threatened city and offered his services to Emperor Leopold. This was the beginning of a long and glorious series of battles and victories at the side of three emperors (Leopold, Joseph I and Charles IV), which made this prince one of the best-loved and most feared men in the empire, backed by the people of Vienna even when the emperor tried in vain to deprive him of his post of commander of the imperial troops, perhaps because the so-called «secret emperor» was beginning to be too important.

It was at the height of this period of glory for the entire empire that baroque art reached its zenith – the visible expression of this power and of a vision of the world that believed in its own strength and its own destiny.

Eugene, grey eminence of the empire, could not help but exert a fundamental role in the field of art and culture as well. When he decided to build a residence in the countryside around Vienna, no less splendid that that of the Hapsburgs, he was stressing his own role in politics and anticipating the «break» in the medieval structure of the city which was to continue uninterruptedly in the following decades, transforming it from a sort of restricted fortress into a great imperial capital.

In 1693, on a tract of land he had bought for the purpose, he entrusted the construction of the palace to one of the most important architects of the time, Johann

Lower Belvedere: facade overlooking the garden.

Lukas von Hildebrandt, who had designed so many baroque buildings in Vienna and who was to accomplish his masterpiece here.

Between 1716 and 1722 work on the two buildings which comprise the residence, the Lower Belvedere and the Upper Belvedere, and the garden, was finished. The prince lived the last years of his life here, surrounded by his books and his astronomical instruments.

Upon the prince's death, after various vicissitudes, the palace became the property of the royal house. Among others, at the beginning of the century it was the residence of Archduke Francis Ferdinand, whose assassination at Sarajevo was the spark that set off World War I.

LOWER BELVEDERE – The Belvedere complex consists of two palaces, set opposite each other and connected by a splendid garden that is on a slight incline. The lower palace, set to all ex-

Lower Belvedere: interior with the «Apotheosis of Prince Eugene».

Upper Belvedere: main facade.

tents and purposes at the foot of a small hill, is known as the Untere Belvedere (Lower Belvedere) and was finished in 1716 and became the effective residence of Prince Eugene.

Two long, almost modest, sober facades conceal sumptuous interiors, a series of rooms and halls richly decorated according to the most classic canons of the baroque. Particular note should be taken of the **Marmorsaal** (Marble hall), frescoed and decorated by Martino Altomonte and Gaetano Fani with scenes which recall moments in the glorious life of the prince.

Right under the arch, entrance to which is from the court of honor in front of the palace, on the right, is the entrance to the two museums which at present occupy the rooms of the palace.

Österreichisches Barockmuseum – The Museum of Austrian Baroque has found its ideal location in these rooms, which provide a perfect setting for the works exhibited. In 9 rooms we find a complete review of the principal artists and artistic trends of 17th- and 18th-century Austria. Among the most important artists mention should be made of G.R. Donner (who executed the sculptures which decorate the Marble Room and the Yellow Room), A. Maulpertsch (for the paintings in rooms 1-4), F.X. Messerschmidt (for the sculpture in the Marble Gallery). The museum preserves, among others, the lead originals of the Donnerbrunnen, the fountain in the Neuer Markt, so-called after the sculptor. The figures represent *Providentia* surrounded by the four rivers *Enns, March, Traun and Ybbs*.

Leaving the palace on the right, one arrives at the «Orangerie» where it is possible to visit the **Museum Mittelalterlicher Österreichischer Kunst** (Museum of Medieval Austrian Art), which exhibits mainly Gothic 15th-century altarpieces and panels in its 5 rooms.

74

THE GARDEN – A large baroque palace could not be considered complete unless it had its garden furnished with the required number of basins, statues and hedges arranged according to the esthetic taste of the time and the stylistic canons of the baroque. The geometric layout of the park follows precise rules: the central axis guides the visitor's eye towards the most important point of the complex system of flower-beds, meadows, decorative elements, from which in turn he can observe the harmonious geometry and the perspective of the whole. Belvedere garden follows the rule. Completed in 1717 by Dominique Girard, it consists of a splendid succession of three grassy terraces which rise towards Upper Belvedere, full of basins, fountains, large waterfalls, flights of stairs and statues representing figures of Greek mythology.

A pleasant walk along the shady paths of this lovely park will take you to the top of the hill. Once there be sure to stop a moment and admire the magnificent panorama of the park and Lower Belvedere with the city in the background.

UPPER BELVEDERE – It would be difficult for Prince Eugene's summer residence to have a lovelier finale than this one. In the Obere Belvedere (Upper Belvedere) von Hildebrandt carried that baroque architecture of which he was one of the masters to its highest levels. The sight of the palace itself is magnificent: a long pavilion with recesses and projections and three rows of windows, striking in its harmony and delicacy of form and in the grandeur of the whole ensemble. Upon entering this pavilion for festive occasions (the building had been designed with this as well as state occasions in mind) one encounters a series of halls and staircases richly decorated with stuccoes, statues and frescoes. The entrance vestibule is particularly suggestive, with the vaults sustained by four powerful pilasters in the form of At-

Upper Belvedere: interior. On the left, staircase of the vestibule; on the right, the «sala terrena» with the Atlantes supporting the vault.

Marmorsaal.

lantes who seem to be holding up the weight of the building. On the first floor one should visit the **Chapel**, frescoed by Carlo Carlone and the **Central Hall**, in red marble, where on May 15, 1955, the treaty between Austria and the forces which occupied it after World War II was ratified, thus re-establishing full Austrian independence and neutrality. The greatest figures of the international political scene of the time participated in this historical event, a real miracle of diplomacy in the midst of the cold war. A painting, hung in the palace, portrays the moment of signing and the participants can all be identified.

Österreichische Galerie des 19. und 20. Jahrhunderts – Today the Upper Belvedere is above all an important gallery of paintings and sculpture. The collection of the Austrian Gallery of 19th and 20th-century art fills over 29 rooms. Some of the important aspects of the great artistic flowering which took place in Vienna between the end of the 19th century and the beginning of the 20th are to be seen. In particular much space is dedicated to the most important artists of the Secession, the movement which came into being in open contrast to the official currents of Austrian art which had been heavily influenced by the imperial taste expressed particularly in the monumental architecture of the Ringstrasse.

Klimt, Schiele, Kokoschka and then, among more recent artists, Fritz Wotruba are only a few of the artists represented in this truly interesting gallery. On the ground floor works created after 1945 (Wotruba) are on exhibit; the first floor is dedicated to portrait painters and Romantic landscape painters of the 19th century (A. Romako, M. Makart, Danhauser and others); the second floor rooms contain paintings and sculpture of the Secession up to 1945 (Klimt, Lienz, Schiele, Kokoschka, Boeckl).

Austrian Gallery of 19th and 20th Century Art:
G. Klimt, «Sonia Knips» (above).
Below: F.G. Waldmüller, «Fronleichnamsmorgen».

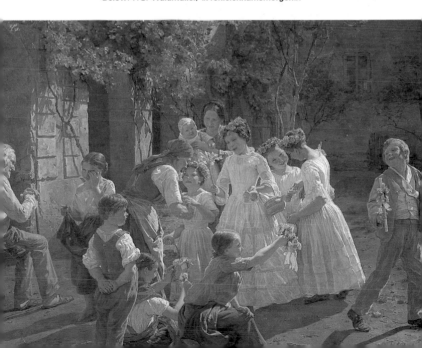

The Kursalon in the Stadtpark where Viennese music is played.

STADTPARK

Opened to the public in 1862, this was the first park built by the City of Vienna. There is a lovely pond with ducks and swans in the meadows. Here and along the banks of the small river Wien one can encounter numerous monuments to famous Viennese, including *Anton Bruckner* and *Franz Schubert*. The most suggestive however is the one to *Johann Strauss*, by E. Hellmer. In the **Kursalon**, a large pavilion at the end of the park, typical Viennese waltzes are played from March to October. The river road is also interesting; particularly the **Wienflussportal** (Gateway of the river Wien), an Art Nouveau kiosk by F. Ohmann, built between 1903 and 1906.

Stadtpark: on the left, monument to Johann Strauss;
on the right, Gateway of the river Wien.

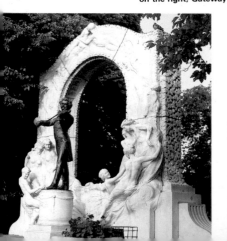

A room in the Museum of Applied Art.

MUSEUM FÜR ANGEWANDTE KUNST

Founded in 1864, the Museum of Applied Art is the oldest museum of its kind in Europe. Thousands of pieces of furniture, utensils, glassware, ceramics, carpets and other objects are collected on two floors in the building on the Stubenring, evidence of the high artistic standards achieved by crafts in different periods and different areas of the world.

The rooms are generally divided chronologically. By following the suggested itinerary, it is possible to take part in an authentic lesson in the history of arts and crafts, and to get a clear picture of the evolution of the styles in relationship to the taste of the time and the techniques available.

Rooms I-II: medieval crafts of the 13th-15th centuries. **Room III**: Renaissance. **Room IV**: Mannerism and the German Renaissance. **Room V**: baroque furniture. **Room VI**: rococo. **Room VII**: Classicism and Biedermeir style. **Room IX**: furniture and objects in Art Nouveau style. **Room XX**: a valuable collection of Oriental rugs. **Room XXII**: glassware and ceramics.

From the museum the Stubenring, and then, on the other bank of the Donaukanal, the Praterstrasse quickly lead to the large park of the Prater. Along the way two important Art Nouveau palaces: on Georg Cock-Platz, which opens off to the left of the Ring, is the tall imposing bulk of the **Postsparkasse** (Post Office Savings Bank) by Otto Wagner, built between 1904 and 1906. Completely restored in the seventies, it is a noteworthy example of functional architecture. The Kassesaal may be visited. A bit further on, along the banks of the canal, next to the Aspern Brücke (Aspern bridge), is the **Urania Palace** built in 1910 by Max Fabiani, a disciple of Wagner's.

PRATER

Not far from the city center and easy to reach by underground, is the Prater, a large park.
In 1560 Emperor Maximilian II transformed this vast tract of land,

The Prater: above, the enormous Riesenrad,
symbol of the city of Vienna; below,
other images of the fabulous Amusement Park.

between the Danube and the Donaukanal, into a hunting reserve to be used exclusively by the court and the aristocracy. Two hundred years later, in 1766, Joseph II, an enlightened soul and a reformer, opened the reserve to the entire population, transforming it into a large park. It soon became the most popular amusement area in Vienna – stands and attractions of all kinds were set up in ever-increasing number and café-chantants opened their doors, transforming its aspect. In the 19th century and up to the fall of the empire, the Prater was a buzzing meeting place, frequented by the Viennese of all social classes.

After the crisis between the two wars and the considerable damage inflicted in 1945, the park today is what it used to be with attractions of various kinds and sport facilities, all immersed in these splendid natural surroundings.

The **Praterstern**, a large rotonda at the beginning of the park in which the subway is located, is the starting point of the **Hauptallee**, the long straight avenue which cuts through the park for all its 5 kilometers of length. At the beginning, on the left, is the **Wurstelprater** (amusement park), the mecca of carousels and amusement park stands, and plentifully supplied with cafés and restaurants. At the entrance is one of the best-known landmarks of the city , the **Riesenrad** (giant wheel) – 67 meters high, with 15 cabins. The wheel turns at a speed of 75 cm a second and offers a magnificent panorama of Vienna. It was built in 1897 by the English engineer W. Basset, who had also designed similar ferris wheels in Chicago, London, Blackpool, and Paris, all of which have long been demolished. Under the wheel is the **Pratermuseum**, which contains relics of the old amusement park that was destroyed in the war in 1945. Not far from the Prater Museum are sport facilities, including the famous football stadium.

Two more views of the Viennese park, a playground for all ages.

KARLSKIRCHE

In 1713 Vienna was struck by the plague for the seventh time. Thousands of citizens were killed by the terrible disease. Emperor Charles VI, preoccupied about the fate of his subjects and his capital, made a vow to consecrate a church in honor of the «plague Saint», St. Charles Borromeo. In 1716, after the plague had ended, Johann B.F. von Erlach began work on the project. At his death a few years later, his son Josef Emanuel took it in hand and finished the building in 1737.

The Church of St. Charles is universally considered one of the masterpieces of baroque art in the field of religious architecture. Seen from the outside, say from the edge of the large artistic basin on which the beautiful but slightly out-of-place sculpture of a *Reclining Figure* by Henry Moore (1977) is set, the church is striking not only for its size but also for the great variety of historical and artistic references embodied in the ensemble.

Facade – Two massive bell towers, each containing a portal, flank the facade. A staircase in the center, with statues on either side, leads towards the six columns of the classical portico with

The massive white Karlskirche.

the principal entrance to the church. In the pediment is a low relief in memory of the *Disasters of the Plague*. But the most surprising architectural elements of the whole complex are the two large columns in front of the porch. The rich spiral relief decorations depict scenes from the life of St. Charles Borromeo, while two fine lanterns crown the summits. A large dome, 72 meters high, dominates the entire building.

Interior – Oval in plan and almost entirely sheathed in marble, the interior of the church is striking in the harmony and symmetry of the forms and the careful studied use of the light that streams in from the large windows in the dome. The *high altar,* by Fischer von Erlach the Elder, is the focal point in an imposing scenography in gold and stucco in which some of the most talented artists of the time collaborated, such as Daniel Gran, Jakob von Schuppen and Sebastiano Ricci. Of particular beauty is a canvas by S. Ricci, painted in 1734, over the second altar to the left, representing the *Assumption of the Virgin*. The high vault of the dome was frescoed by J. Michael Rottmayr between 1725 and 1730 with the *Glory of St. Charles.*

KARLSPLATZ

This spacious tree-lined square, which barely extends beyond the Ring, is connected to the center of the city by Kärntnerstrasse and is one of the hub points for Viennese culture, as well as being one of the principal traffic junctions. Around a series of gardens, basins and monuments (including one to **Johannes Brahms**), buildings and institutions which have played an important role in the great artistic flowering of 19th- and 20th-century Vienna alternate with baroque masterpieces such as the Church of St. Charles, an example of the splendor of the Hapsburg Empire in the 18th century.

Upon leaving the church and turning right to skirt the square one encounters first the building of the Historisches Museum der Stadt Wien (Historical Museum of the city of Vienna), followed by the Musikvereingebäude (Building of the Society of the Friends of Music), the Künstlerhaus (Artists' House) and the pavilions of the old transportation system. In Friedrichstrasse, which lies opposite the church, is the Sezessionhaus (Secession House), temple of Viennese Art Nouveau.

HISTORISCHES MUSEUM DER STADT WIEN

The Historical Museum of the city of Vienna, opened to the public in 1959, provides an excellent occasion to get to know the history of the city and its development and to better one's understanding of the significance of the city's various monuments. The museum is laid out on three floors of a modern building and includes finds and evidence of more than 2000 years of history.

Ground floor – It is dedicated to the period that goes from prehistory to the 15th century. Artifacts from the ancient settlements on the banks of the Danube and the fortified Roman encampment of «Vindobona» are on exhibit as well as articles relat-

Karlsplatz: on the left, monument to Johannes Brahms; on the right, pavilion of the transportation system built by Otto Wagner in the early 1900s.

ed to the Vienna of the Babenbergs and the construction of the large religious buildings of the 14th and 15th centuries (material and plans having to do with St. Stephen's).

First floor – It is dedicated to the 16th and 17th centuries. Objects from the war against the Turks (suits of armor, weapons, flags captured in the two sieges of 1529 and 1683), a model of the city before its walls were demolished, paintings and art objects of the 18th century.

Second floor – This part deals with the Vienna of the 19th and 20th centuries, the modern city. A room with its original furniture, memoir of the great Austrian poet Franz Grillparzer, has been preserved as well as paintings and works by neoclassic, Romantic and Art Nouveau artists. Contemporary artists represented include Klimt, Kokoschka, Schiele, Wotruba and Boeckl. There is also another model of 19th-century Vienna after the construction of the Ring.

MUSIKVEREIN

Built between 1867 and 1869 by T. Hansen, the Building of the Society of the Friends of Music is today one of the centers for musical activities in Vienna. The heart of this large building, which also houses a fine collection of musical instruments, is the large **concert hall**: 51 meters long, 19 meters wide, with a capacity of 2000 persons. Its acoustics are among the best to be found in concert halls throughout the world. The atmosphere too is magical with the sumptuous decoration of the walls and ceilings and the great hanging chandeliers.
This is the hall from which the famous «New Year's Concert» is broadcast throughout the world every year on January first, executed by the Philharmonic Orchestra of Vienna, one of the most prestigious symphony orchestras in the world whose official seat is in this building.

Near the Musikverein is the **Künstlerhaus** (Artists' House), a building erected in 1868 which for a long time was the «official» gallery of the academic artists. The Secession movement, led by Gustav Klimt, was the answer to this classicizing and imitative art. Important temporary exhibitions are now held here.

TRANSPORTATION SYSTEM PAVILIONS

When the new underground transportation system was under construction at the beginning of the seventies, the two pavilions of the old tram system (urban transport system), which Otto Wagner had designed and built at the beginning of the

**Secession House with its distinctive dome
of gilded laurel leaves.**

century, were renovated. Together with other stations (Schönbrunn, Kettenbrük-
kengasse, Stadtpark, Roussauer Lände), the two pavilions in Karlsplatz are a fine
example of Art Nouveau architecture, of which Wagner was a master. These two
pavilions are particularly sumptuous, made of iron, copper, marble and gold for the
decorations, and characterized by a remarkable esthetic feeling for detail. One of
the buildings is now used as entrance to the subway, while the other is a café and
the branch office of the Historical Museum of the City of Vienna.

SECESSION HOUSE

In 1897 a group of artists, including G. Klimt, K. Moser, K. Moll,
J. Olbrich and J. Hoffmann, in open disagreement with the official artistic movements of the Academy, organized a new movement called «Austrian Secession» to sustain and give incentive

**Secession House: on the left, metal doorway by G. Klimt;
on the right, bronze monument to Marcus Antonius.**

to new art expressions. For this purpose they also had a new exposition center built. The Viennese Jugendstil or Art Nouveau found its ideal headquarters in this building. Constructed between 1897 and 1898, it was designed by Joseph Olbrich, who was also responsible for the iron **dome** in the form of laurel leaves which puts a finishing touch on the essential geometric lines of the building. The metal parts of the structure are by G. Klimt. On the facade is the motto of the movement: «To each time its own art. To each art its freedom». Next to Secession House is the **monument to Marcus Antonius** by A. Strasser (1899).

AKADEMIE DER BILDENDEN KÜNSTE

Right behind the Friedrichstrasse, a stone's throw from Karlsplatz, a fine square in Renaissance style, Schillerplatz (with a monument to the great poet at the center), is the site of the building of the Academy of Fine Arts, founded in 1692 and installed in this edifice designed by T. Hansen around 1876. It is the oldest academy in German-speaking countries and the only one, in this ambience, which has a **Picture Gallery**. The gallery contains works by the major exponents of European art, from the 16th to the 17th century. Among others: Hieronymus Bosch (*triptych of the Last Judgement*); Titian (*Tarquin and Lucrezia*); Rubens (*Circumcision*); F. Guardi (*eight Views of Vienna*); Luca Giordano (*Judgement of Paris*); Memling (*Crucifixion*); P. de Hooch (*Dutch Family*); Murillo (*Boys at Play*); Van Dyck (*Self-Portrait*); Van Ruisdael (*Landscape*). There are also works by G.B. Tiepolo, Rembrandt, S. Miel and many others, in particular of the Dutch and Flemish schools. The academy also has a rich **Print Cabinet**, with about 100,000 items including drawings, water colors, engravings, lithographs and woodcuts.

LINKE WIENZEILE

A long street begins at Karlsplatz at the level of the Secession House and continues up to Schönbrunn and beyond. This is the Linke Wienzeile, a lively center of Viennese folklore as well as the place where various particularly interesting buildings are to be found.
Almost at the beginning of the street, at n. 6, is the **Theater an der Wien**. Inaugurated in 1801, the first performance of Beethoven's «Fidelio» was held here (1805) and Beethoven himself also lived here briefly. After him, many other composers had the premier performances of their works in this theater. At present the classical Viennese operettas are generally programmed. Opposite the theater, in the area which divides the Linke Wienzeile from its twin, the Rechte Wienzeile, is where the **Naschmarkt** begins. This is a picturesque lively food market which caters to all tastes with exotic products including spices and herbs. There are many refreshment booths among the stands. The **Flohmarkt** (Flea Market) is held every Saturday at the end of the Naschmarkt. An occasional interesting find may turn up among the curios on sale in this typical bazaar of second-hand objects.

The imaginative facade of the Majolikahaus.

Anyone who intends to buy something in this small but densely crowded market had better come early. The best things will obviously be the first to disappear and latecomers are left with a pile of useless objects. An ideal place to stop after the market is the café «Wienzeile», a characteristic Viennese spot that is crowded on market days.

Opposite the Flohmarkt, are two splendid examples of Art Nouveau architecture, both by Otto Wagner (1898). At n. 40 is the **Majolikahaus**, its facade faced with tiles that are decorated with elaborate floral motifs in various colors. N. 38 is another private house, decorated on the outside with gilded medallions designed by Kolo Moser. In both cases a great deal of attention has been paid to the details of the exterior and the interior, such as the balconies, the iron railings, or the small columns which support the terraces of Majolikahaus. One cannot help but admire this combination of richness and elegance, clearly in contrast with the solemn redundant style of so many official palaces of the same period.

An elegant building on the Linke Wienzeile.

SPITTELBERG QUARTER

A pleasant walk through the streets of the VI (Mariahilf) and the VII (Neubau) districts leads to the Spittelberg, an old quarter situated behind Maria Theresienplatz.

Enemy artillery often chose this little hill right outside the city walls as an ideal site from which to bombard Vienna. The Turks did so in 1683 and the French in 1809. With the urban development of the 18th century this area, too, was turned into a building zone and it became one of the most infamous quarters of the city, full of taverns and all kinds of shady commerce. As the years went by the quarter fell into such a state of decay and abandon that the authorities found themselves faced with one of two decisions – either demolish it completely or recuperate the architectural heritage. Fortunately, the latter choice prevailed in the seventies, thanks also to the pressure exerted by vast sectors of public opinion. Today Spittelberg is a charming ensemble of lanes, buildings, courtyards, all perfectly restored, full of meeting places, craft shops, good restaurants. Some of the streets have been closed to traffic, creating an excellent alternative for a promenade and shopping right outside the historical center. The **Spittelberggasse**, a pedestrian zone with a pleasant square surrounded by restaurants and cafés, is the heart of this area which hides its most characteristic features in the thousand internal courtyards of the houses. A fine example of this is the **Amerlinghaus** (in Stiftgasse n. 8), seat of an active cultural center, with an adjacent tavern which uses the courtyard of the house.

The courtyard of the baroque house
on St. Ulrichsplatz.

The **St. Ulrichskirche** (Church of St. Ulrich), built between 1721 and 1724 on the site of two older chapels which date back to the 13th century, faces on the adjacent Burggasse. But the surrounding piazza itself is more interesting than the church, as is the **baroque house**, at n. 2 on the square. Built in the middle of the 18th century, it may be one of the best examples of its kind in all of Vienna, with its ornate facade, the magnificent courtyard, the balconies which connect the various apartments, the small internal pavilion, all constituting an ensemble of rare beauty, even in a city as full of baroque works of art as Vienna.

Continuing along Langegasse one arrives at the center of the VIII district (Josefstadt). At n. 34, a fine baroque house, is the café «Alte Backstube», which in addition to the traditional delicacies offered by Viennese cafés, houses an odd **Bread Museum**, with utensils, forms and containers for flour which date back to the Middle Ages. A crossing, Maria Treugasse, leads to the Jodok Fink-Platz, the splendid setting for the Church of the Piarists.

PIARISTENKIRCHE MARIA TREU

Built on designs by J.L. von Hildebrandt, in 1716, it dominates the square with its yellow ocher facade flanked by two bell towers 76 meters high. Inside note should be taken of the *frescoes* in the dome and the ceiling, by Franz Anton Maulbertsch, representing the Virgin and scenes from the Bible, and the painting over the tabernacle, *Maria Treu* by J. Herz (1713) from which the church takes its name.

In the square is a column to the Virgin (Mariensäule) by J. Prokop, commissioned by a noble who thus expressed his thanks to the Virgin for the end of the plague of 1713.

PALAIS LIECHTENSTEIN

Moving to the IX district (Alsergrund), by car or bus, one reaches the Palais Liechtenstein, situated between Liechtensteinstrasse and the Porzellangasse.
Built between 1698 and 1711 on plans by D. Martinelli, it is considered one of the loveliest baroque palaces in the city. The simple facade conceals an interior with a wealth of decorations and frescoes. Mention should be made of the fresco by A. Pozzo in the central hall which represents the *Apotheosis of Hercules*, the stuccoes and frescoes by J.M. Rottmayr in the ground floor hall, and the works by S. Bussi, A. Bellucci and J.B. Prokop in the other rooms of the palace. Since 1979 the Museum of Modern Art has been housed here.

Museum für Moderne Kunst – Almost all the great names of contemporary painting are represented in 15 rooms. They range from the great names of the Austrian Secession to the most recent representatives of avant-garde artists. The museum's most important section is without doubt that of «Art of the last thirty years», representing the latest artistic tendencies: Natural, surreal or fantastic realism, Happenings, Pop Art, Photorealism, Geometric abstraction. Many of the exhibited pieces come from the collection of Ludwig of Aachen. The more prestigous names are Klimt, Schiele, Kokoschka, Kandinsky, Mondrian, Max Ernst, Magritte, Picasso, Léger, Klee, Miró, A. Masson, Lucio Fontana, Dubuffet, Warhol, Roy Lichtenstein, Botero, as well as many contemporary Austrian artists.

JOSEPHINUM

Not far from Palais Liechtenstein, in Währinger Strasse at n. 25, the 18th-century **Military Academy of Surgery and Medicine** (built between 1783 and 1785 by I. Canevale) keeps a prodigious and disquieting collection of anatomical wax models in the **Museum des Instituts für Geschichte der Medizin**. The models were prepared in 1775 on the order of Emperor Joseph II, as a teaching aid for the surgeons in his imperial army, all too often «awkward» when called upon to operate on wounded soldiers. Florentine craftsmen (it is no coincidence that Florence has a similar collection) constructed mannequins of men and women with open abdomens in which the viscera could be clearly seen, or who were accurately flayed to show the muscles and the arteries and veins. The melancholy sweetness of these wax faces haunts the visitor, contrasting inevitably with the verisimilitude of these rent bodies.

SIGMUND FREUD HAUS

In Berggasse another house-museum bears witness to Vienna's importance in the field of contemporary scientific thought. The **Sigmund Freud Museum** has been set up in the house where the founder of psychoanalysis lived for fifty years. These rooms, this furniture, witnessed the development and classification of the revolutionary Freudian theories on the psyche and human behavior, at least until 1938 when the arrival of the Nazis forced the scientist to seek refuge elsewhere.

THE SUBURBS OF THE CITY

MUSEUM DES 20. JAHRHUNDERTS – In the garden facing the Sud-Bahnhof, is the Museum of the Twentieth Century. Planned in 1958 by Karl Schwanzer as the Austrian pavilion for the World's Fair in Brussels, it reached it's final location only after being completely dismantled and transported to Vienna. Sculptures of bronze and stone decorate the courtyards and gardens. Among these are works by Moore, Giacometti, Wotruba, Wander Bertoni; at the entrance is Aristide Maillol's sculpture of 1905, the powerful *Die gefesselte Kraft*.

HEERESGESCHICHTLICHES MUSEUM

Next to the Museum of the Twentieth Century is the Historic Arms Museum, built in 1850-56 by Theophil Hansen and Ludwig Förster in a Roman-Byzantine style. It is housed inside the arsenal that Francis Joseph had built (1849-55) by Eduard van der Nüll and August von Siccardsburg on the site of a preceding arsenal. Paintings, arms, documents, banners and uniforms reconstruct the military history of Austria from the Thirty Years' War to World War I. Warranting particular mention, besides the grand exposition of pieces of 16th- to 18th-century artillery, are the suit of armour of Prince Eugene, a Turkish tent, an aerostat from 1796 and the automobile on board which, on June 28, 1914, the archduke Ferdinand, heir to the Hapsburg Empire, became the victim of the Sarajevo assassination.

Army Museum: on the left, atrium of the Museum; on the right, Maria Theresa room, Turkish tent.

**Monumental cemetery of St. Mark's: the tomb
of Wolfgang Amadeus Mozart.**

ST. MARX FRIEDHOF – At Leberstrasse n. 3, a bit isolated from the principal
avenues of circulation and almost suffocated by a recently constructed viaduct, is
the monumental cemetery of St. Mark's, used as such until the mid-19th century.
Open from April to October, and now more garden than cemetery it becomes
particularly suggestive in May when all its lilies are in full bloom. It was here in 1791,
that Wolfgang Amadeus Mozart was buried in a common plot. A rather lachrymose
corner marks the anonymous burial place of this great artist, whose remains can
never be recovered.

ZENTRALFRIEDHOF – The extant cemeteries soon proved inadequate when the
great urban development of Vienna began in the 19th century. In 1874 the new
Zentralfriedhof (Central Cemetery, IX district) was inaugurated. Before long this
great funerary garden was to become one of the most famous monumental cemeteries in Europe. From the large Art Nouveau gateway built in 1905 by Max Eegele,
the tree-lined avenue leads to the area of the tombs of «Austria's great», an authentic mausoleum of men of culture and of the most prestigious politicians of the country including the tombs of Ludwig van Beethoven, Schubert, Brahms, J. Strauss,
father and son, Hugo Wolf, Arnold Schönberg, the crypt of the presidents of the
Austrian Republic and a mausoleum in honor of Wolfgang Amadeus Mozart.

Left, Zentralfriedhof; right, Kirche am Steinhof.

Modern complex known as UNO-City.

KIRCHE AM STEINHOF – This is one of the masterpieces of Viennese Art Nouveau. The first thing one sees from afar is the copper dome of the Church of Steinhof built in the city's XIV district by Otto Wagner between 1903 and 1907. In building it Wagner paid attention to every detail: from the overall structure, simple yet refined, with its white walls, and its rigorously geometric lines, to the interior, richly decorated with motifs and images in which the dominant color is gold. The *mosaic stained-glass windows* by Kolo Moser are also lovely.

KARL MARX-HOF - Between the two wars the city government of Vienna was controlled by the socialists who set in motion an impressive building policy of new low-cost apartments in their attempt to solve the dramatic problems of providing housing for all the citizens. Of the 64,000 apartments built in that period, the enormous complex of the Karl Marx-Hof in the XIX district is outstanding. With its over 1600 apartments it provides living quarters for over 5,000 people.
The facade, 1200 meters long and scanned by six towers, is one of the symbols of the so-called «red Vienna» of the twenties and thirties. It is considered an example of expressionist architecture, with touches of cubist and Art Déco influence. It was built between 1927 and 1930 by Karl Ehn, a pupil of Otto Wagner's. The fields and gardens which surround the building should also be noted.

INTERNATIONALE ZENTRUM WIEN – Also known as **UNO-City** (United Nations City) it is the symbol both of Austrian neutrality and of Austria's new international role as the center of the meeting between East and West and North and South.
Built in the XXII district between 1973 and 1979, this gigantic complex of glass, steel and cement houses offices of international organizations such as the international agency for atomic energy, the organization for industrial development (UNIDO) and the center for social development and for humanitarian affairs.
Situated along the Danube, near the Donaupark, it is characterized by its four large office towers which are 120, 100, 80 and 60 meters high, with 24,000 windows to illuminate the rooms of the more than 3000 employees.

DONAUPARK – In 1964 this area of the XXII district, between the Danube and the «Old Danube» – an arm of the river which no longer is connected to the river itself – was transformed into a fine park furnished with artificial lakes, playgrounds for children, public establishments and an ice skating rink. The 252 meters of the **Donauturm** (Donau Tower) rise over the park. It was modelled on the television towers so common in many other cities and was built in 1964 for the International Garden Exhibition in Vienna. Swift elevators take one to a turning café-restaurant, 170 meters up, with a panorama of the city and the river.

The picturesque streets of Grinzing
with their numerous taverns.

HEURIGEN

«Heurige» is the most recently made wine which is sold in the establishments on the outskirts of Vienna, where the city melts into the surrounding countryside, in what were small villages which have been absorbed by the metropolis.
Each of these wine-shops, run by the producers themselves, is marked by a green branch that is hung outside. Food is also served, all to the accompaniment of traditional music. A visit to a Heurigenschänke has become the thing to do evenings for both the Viennese and tourists. These establishments are to be found in all the outer suburban districts of Vienna. Some of the most famous are listed below.

Grinzing – This is the best known locality. About twenty wine-shops are open here as well as many other establishments where one can eat and where music is played. Situated in the XIX district, the Heurigenschänke are concentrated around a few picturesque streets. From Grinzing, via Cobenzlgasse, one can reach the Höhenstrasse, a stupendous panoramic route which winds along the slopes of the Wiener Wald and, touching on Kahlenberg, ends at Leopoldsberg. The name **Kahlenberg** is closely bound to the Turkish siege of Vienna and the defeat inflicted on

The gay and animated Heurigenschänke in suburban Vienna.

**Two other places in the immediate vicinity: on the left,
Kahlenberg, Josefskirche; on the right,
Leopoldsberg, baroque church.**

the Turks by the imperial troups together with those of the Polish king, John Sobies-
ky. A splendid view of Vienna and the Danube can be had from the panoramic terrace of the restaurant near the 18th-century Josefskirche (Church of St. Joseph).
Even more extensive and evocative is the panorama to be seen from the belvedere
of the **Leopoldberg**, on a cliff overhanging the river and set in front of the small Leo-
poldskirche (Church of Leopold) built in 1679 by Leopold I.

Heiligenstadt - Nussdorf – This locality is in the XIX district too and is known as
a vacation site and a place for outings. L. van Beethoven sojourned for a long time
– between 1802 and 1824 – in a house in Heiligenstadt.

Stammersdorf – In the XXI district, beyond the Danube, it is the most important
production zone in Vienna, with over 100 wine-producers and about 40 Heurigenschänke. Hagenbrunnerstrasse, better known as Kellergasse «Wine cellar street»
is picturesque with its wine shops which are really nothing but the kitchens and gardens of the farmers' houses, surrounded by green fields and vineyards.
Other localities where Heurigenschänke can be found are Strebesdorf, Sievering,
Neustift am Walde, Hernals, Ottakring, Mauer, Oberlaa.

Ludwig van Beethoven's house in Heiligenstadt-Nussdorf.

INDEX

Stearer Ich Restaurant